MW01138229

J D Stockholm

J D STOCKHOLM

The ADventures oF
StupiD Boy
AnD
mr TeD

What readers are saying:

"Fresh writing style."

"… a sobering look into the terrifying world of child abuse as seen through the survivor's eyes… a five-year-old boy."

"The reader is easily transported."

"I found myself praying for him throughout the book. I found myself cursing and talking out loud and comforting him."

"… then there was his childlike vocabulary, his bright mind, his utterly sweet spirit, even his ignorance of what was actually happening on every level, it was all like a buffer against the horror of it."

J D STOCKHOLM

Based on a true story. However, some things may
have been changed for clarity, and of course
names and places have been changed for privacy.

ISBN-13:978-1481895613
ISBN-10:1481895613

Other Works.

Dear Teddy – Journal of a Boy book one

Available at Amazon.com and Amazon.co.uk

Telling Teddy – Journal of a Boy book two

Available at Amazon.com and Amazon.co.uk

Dark Ramblings of the Phoenix

Available at Amazon.com and Amazon.co.uk

Contact

dearmrted@gmail.com

http://jdstockholm.com/

http://www.facebook.com/dearmrted

ONE

There was a boy. His name was Stupid Boy. He had a stupid cape and stupid boots and he looked stupid with his stupid hair. He lived in a house that was by the sea with no mum and dad because no one wanted to live with Stupid Boy. They got to laugh at him and call him names.

His mum and dad didn't let him live in their house too because they didn't like him. No one in the whole wide world liked Stupid Boy.

Stupid boy lived with a lady. She didn't get to be stupid like him. She was nice and kind. She was the only one that liked Stupid Boy.

Stupid Boy wanted to be like Superman. He got a cape one day and tried to fly. But the cape didn't work because stupid boys don't get to fly.

Stupid Boy wanted to be a secret spy. But he didn't be able to do that because he didn't be very good at spying on things. He had to make his stupids go away.

One day, Stupid Boy and the Lady went into town to buy some things. It got to be a rainy day and Stupid Boy forgot his coat. He got all wet when the rain got through his clothes. He closed his eyes and he made a big wish.

"Maybe the rain will make my stupids go away," he said. He closed his eyes tight and then he wished the hardest he ever could.

The rain didn't make his stupids go away.

STUPID BOY

Stupid Boy and the Lady went in the shops because the Lady needed to buy food. Stupid Boy ate it all up because he was too greedy and so she had to buy more and more. Maybe the shop would sell beans. Like the ones that Jack got for his beanstalk. But not beans that were green and growed up into the sky. Maybe beans that jumped and made Stupid Boy not be stupid any more.

Stupid Boy asked the Lady for some jumping beans. She said yes and bought him some.

Stupid Boy got the magic beans. But they didn't grow beanstalks and they didn't make him jump all the way in the sky. The beans just jumped about in his hands. Stupid Boy put them in his pocket.

When the food was all bought and then it got into bags. The Lady asked Stupid Boy if he could be a good boy and help her carry them home. Stupid Boy knew how to pretend to be a good boy. He said yes and then he got a bag and carried it.

Stupid Boy's legs got tired on the way home. He got an idea. A big fat stupid idea. He asked the Lady if he could hold her hand when they walked. She said yes. Stupid Boy held the Lady's hand and they walked. Stupid Boy closed his eyes. Maybe he could sleepwalk and the Lady didn't let him walk into the road.

Stupid boy stepped on the cracks. Everyone knew if you step on the cracks makes you fall and break your back.

Stupid Boy falled over and bashed his knee.

Stupid Boy falled over and everyone got to see.

Because he was stupid.

The Lady knew how to make Stupid Boy better. It didn't be the medicine his mum got him. That didn't work. The Lady decided that to make his stupids go away they had to chop off his head with a big axe. Then he didn't be Stupid Boy anymore.

The End.

I have my book and my big black felt-tip pen; I draw Stupid Boy with his stupid hair and his stupid shoes. I get the stapler. I make it go through the paper. I make Stupid Boy's eyes and nose and all his hair. I do it lots of times all messy because Stupid Boy has big messy hair. I do it wrong though. I don't know my finger is there and then it staples my finger through the paper.

"See?"

I am Stupid Boy. I tell Mr. Ted. "Stupid, stupid, big fat Stupid Boy."

Maybe my Nan can get my head chopped off and give me a new one that isn't stupid. Then everyone will like me and I won't be stupid anymore.

I don't show my Nan my finger. She will know I am Stupid Boy too and then maybe she will go away like my mum did. Then she won't want me anymore because I am just bad inside.

STUPID BOY

I don't let the tears go down my stupid face either. It's good when it gets to hurt lots. Sometimes, I make it hurt on purpose. Maybe it will make all the stupid parts go away. I get my scissors and I pick the staple. It is stuck in my finger. It hurts. But that's what stupid boys get.

That's why my mum doesn't want me. Because I am stupid. I keep asking her. She tells me they don't have any bed for me so I don't be able to live there. I sleep at their house sometimes. On the weekends. But I don't sleep on a bed. I sleep on my mum's sun chair in their bedroom. My dad gave me his sleeping bag to keep me warm.

No one wanted me. Just like Stupid Boy. All alone and stinky. Me and Mr. Ted sit on the wall outside lots of times. Not the wall at my Nan's house. It's a wall at the end of the road. Mr. and Mrs. Robinson live there. They don't tell us off for sitting on the wall. We sit there all the time. I try and tell my mum in my brain that I'm sorry. "Please come back," I say, but she never does. Not ever.

My Nan tells me to stop sitting on the wall.

"Maybe you'll make the wall all bumpy from your bottom," she says.

But I am not all big and heavy. My Nan is silly. She tells me to come back into the house because it is cold and I will catch a chill. I don't want to. I want to wait for my mum and dad to come back for me. They are going to. When they miss me lots inside then my mum will tell my dad to drive the car and come and get me. Then she will say she is sorry and they will take me home with them. It is okay I don't have a bed. I can sleep in the chair forever.

STUPID BOY

TWO

One day, Stupid Boy waked up when it was all bright and early. He had to go to school.
Stupid Boy jumped out of bed. It was a special day. He got very excited. He got to have a sleepover at his mum and dad's house.

The End.

My Nan makes me breakfast. I eat it all up and then I go to school. I don't get dressed very good. The shoes are all small and they make my toes squish up. My socks have holes in them. I look stupid.

I don't talk to anyone all day long. I sit at my table in the classroom. It is numbers day. I don't use my fingers very good to count. They are sore from when I got them stapled together.

I need to go to the toilet. I don't be allowed to go. I have to ask. I stick my hand all big in the sky and I ask my teacher if I can go. She says yes.

I stand up to go to the toilet. The bad man is at the door. He makes me scared in my tummy. I didn't ever see him at school before. He has his bad smile at me. I squeeze my eyes all tight and shut then he can't see me because I go invisible. Me and Mr. Ted have been practising.

"Make the bad man go away," I say.

I know the bad man has come because I am so stupid that I got my fingers stapled together.

Then he has to hurt me to make all my stupid go away forever.

But I am so stupid. I stand there and the scared in my tummy makes me pee my pants. It goes down my leg.

Stupid stinky boy. Stupid stinky boy that is a big fat baby.

Maybe my teacher can chop off my head. She can chop me into lots of bits and then all the puppies in the area can have a bit. That's what my dad says when he sings his song because I tell tales. That's what happens.

I don't know why the bad man had got to the school and I don't know why I got to wet my pants. I stand there. I don't see the bad man anymore. Maybe it is my brain and all the stupid pictures. It shows them to me lots of times and then they make me jump and all scared inside.

The teacher sees that I wet my pants. She holds my hand and then says that we have to go to the library where it is all very quiet. Maybe she will put a nappy on me because I am so stupid that I wet my pants like a big fat baby.

The teacher is nice. She is called Mrs. Richardson. She has flowers in her hair and on her dress. She smells pretty too. Not like me. I am stinky. Now I am stinky like pee.

"Is there something wrong?" she asks me.

But I shake my head and I don't tell her about the bad man. I don't tell her that I am the stupidest in the whole wide world that the bad man even comes to school to get me. I fold my arms and then shake my head. I tell her with my brain that I am just stupid inside.

Stupid Stinky Boy that pees in his pants.

I go home at home time. Mrs. Richardson gives me a note that I have to give to my Nan. Then my Nan will get to know why I have different pants on and not mine. She gets to know that I get my pants wet. Maybe she will get mad about it. My mum will get mad about it.

"More damn cleaning," she always says.

That's all I ever make her do. Lots of damn cleaning.

I forgot my coat. That is what I have to say to my Nan. But I didn't. I left it in the cloak room because I didn't want to go in there in case the bad man was hiding there. Maybe it doesn't be my brain showing me pictures. Maybe it is really him and he is there. Then he will do the hurt thing and make me cry and get the scratches and bite me because I am so bad. No one ever likes me. Maybe the bad man can chop me all into millions of bits and then chop my head off and throw it away.

Maybe the bad man is like magic and he gets to make himself invisible.

I don't tell my Nan about the bad man. I say I forgot my coat because I am excited in my tummy. It is Friday and I am going for a sleepover at my mum and dad's house like I did with Graham.

My Nan says it is okay. She doesn't get mad about it. She tells me that I shouldn't tell my mum.

"She'll get mad and it doesn't matter. You can get it on Monday."

I tell my Nan that I won't. I tell Mr. Ted though. Because I have to tell him about the bad man at school. Maybe Mr. Ted knows why he is there.

Me and Mr. Ted sit and wait for my mum and dad. My Nan doesn't be allowed to give me any dinner when I am going for a sleepover.

My mum says, "You're my child, not hers, and I'll feed you myself."

Sometimes, my mum forgets about the dinner part. But it is okay. I get big food at school and I don't be very hungry in the night time.

My mum says she is going to get me when my dad gets to finish work. But he finished a long time ago. Maybe I am stupid and I don't know the time. Or maybe I get the day wrong. I ask my Nan if it is Friday and she says it is.

"Is my mum coming?" I ask her, and she nods her head and says yes.

"Maybe they are just a little late with your dad at work," she says.

I get to try and hear with my ears. I listen real hard. Maybe I will get to hear their car when they come. Then I can get my boots on and we can go to their new house. It takes forever. I get to look at the clock. It is all the way past the eight. My mum says she is going to get me when the little hand is at the bottom which is the six and then the big hand gets to be at the top. That means it is six o'clock and then they will come. But the little hand is on the eight.

Maybe they forgot.

I get the sad feeling in my tummy. I don't even tell Mr. Ted about it. I don't want to tell anyone ever. If I keep it a secret maybe they will come and get me. But I don't know how to make the sad feeling stay away. I try to think about lots of nice things. But my brain doesn't want to. I wish my mum and dad get to come soon.

The little hand gets on the nine. Then I get to hear the car door make a slam noise outside. I get up fast like Superman. I get my boots on and all my things and I don't forget Mr. Ted because he gets to come too. I get a big smile on my face and I am happy that I get to see my mum and dad.

I give my Nan the biggest hug ever and kiss. I tell her I will see her Sunday and she says yes and tells me to be a good boy.

I will. I will.

I leave the stupids in the bed and then I just get to be good all weekend.

My dad comes into the backroom. He gets his angry eyes on. Maybe he gets to know about my coat or my pants that I get wet. But he doesn't get mad.

"Come on," he says and I do.

I follow him to the car and wave bye-bye to my Nan. She gets to stand at the door and wave at me.

I get to go to my mum and dad's. I get to sit in the car. It is a long-long way away. It is in the forest with all the farms and the fields with the cows and the sheep. They live on a road that is all bumpy because of the big tractors. It is very dark when we get to the house.

The house has a big giant driveway made of bumpy stones. I make a noise when the car gets to bump along, but my dad tells me to shut up.

My mum says that it is already bedtime. My brother is tired. They have been late because they went to the cinema and then they went to get dinner and it has taken a long time. I don't get any dinner. My mum has forgotten. I don't tell her. I am not hungry anyway. I tell Mr. Ted in my brain that it is okay. We can wait until breakfast time.

My dad says he is tired too and maybe me and my brother want to go to bed and read a story book. I tell him yes please and I smile really big.

THREE

One day, Stupid Boy was playing by the pond. He found an egg.

It was not an ordinary egg, Stupid Boy thought. Maybe it was magic. Stupid Boy didn't know.

Stupid Boy asked his mum what the egg was. She looked at it and shaked her head. She didn't know.

Stupid Boy asked his dad what the egg was.

"I'm not sure," his dad said. "Maybe it is a duck egg?"

A duck egg? That made Stupid Boy very excited indeed.

A magic duck egg.

Maybe there was a magic duck. Maybe magic ducks could talk.

The End

"I'm going to keep you all warm and safe," I say to the egg. I put it in my pocket.

"What do you do to look after an egg?"

I had done it at school with chicks.

Something to keep it in.

I find a box.

Something to keep it warm.

I find some blankets.

How long to keep the egg all warm? I don't know.

I know that eggs have to be turned over lots of times in the day.

But who would turn the egg over when I go back home?

I ask my mum. She says no.

I ask my dad. He says okay.

I draw pictures for the magic duck. The magic duck that gets to talk. I put them in my book. I will show magic duck when he hatches.

I make my dad promise that he will look after the egg when I am gone. My dad says he will.

It is a week later and I get my sleepover for the weekend. I can't wait to see the magic duck. Maybe he has hatched.

The magic duck is not hatched yet. The egg has a big crack in it. The baby duck is dead. I am Stupid Boy. I hug the box and cry about magic duck that got to be dead.

Poor magic duck.

I don't tell my dad about the duck. He will say that I did it and that I am stupid. I don't want him to say those words. They make me all sad inside. I am sad about the duck. It makes my tummy feel bad. He is just a little duck and now he is dead. I put the egg in the pond and then no one gets to see it.

Stupid Boy didn't hatch the egg.

My dad reads to me when it is bedtime. He does the hurt thing. I am glad he makes it hurt.

Then maybe next time I don't make the duck all dead. I lie on my sun chair and watch the door. Maybe the bad man will come too because I make the duck dead.

I wake up again in the morning time. My mum and dad say we are going out. They wake my brother up too. It is all nice and early. My mum tells me to go and make the table nice for breakfast. Then I get to sit in the other room because they have forgot to buy breakfast again. It is okay.

Stupid Boys don't eat breakfast.

I get Mr. Ted, but I don't say any words to him. I tell him we are going out somewhere in my brain. He doesn't know where it is too. Maybe it is somewhere nice. I don't know. I don't want to go.

I don't be allowed to take Mr. Ted with me in the car. My mum says he will get dirty and then maybe they will throw him in the bin. I don't want Mr. Ted to go in the bin so I leave him at the dining table and tell him to be good.

I ask my mum where we are going.

"Shut up and stop asking questions," she says.

I wish I have my story book. Then I can write about Stupid Boy that always makes his mum be mad at him because he says all the stupid things. Stupid Boy has to learn to stop it. Then maybe his mum will ask him to live with them in the big house. The big house has seven bedrooms in it. They can put the sun chair in one of the rooms and then Stupid Boy can get to live with his mum and dad like all the other children do.

We drive all the way back over the bridge and nearly to where my Nan's house is. But then we don't go there. I am scared because maybe they are going to take me home. Maybe they are sick of me. Maybe my dad knows that I have made the magic duck dead and he is going to take me back. But he doesn't. We get to drive past and maybe I can say hello to my Nan. But we don't stop.

We go to a place; it is down lots of lanes and things. There are lots and lots of giant big houses. Maybe it is where all the rich people get to live. There is a gate at the end and it is a place for animals. It has a big sign at the front. It is a place for animals that don't get a place to live. I have never seen one before. But I know the name because my Nan got her cat from here.

They put all the animals here when no one wants them. Maybe there is one for children too. Maybe if my Nan doesn't ever want me I can get to a place like this and be on sale.

There are lots of animals and they are all in cages. We talk to the man at the door and then he says we can look at a dog and that she is ready.

"You stay here," my mum says to me.

I have to stay by the car. My brother is all excited and he holds my mum's hand. He doesn't be able to stop talking about a dog.

STUPID BOY

My brother gets a big dog. She is big and gold. Her name is Sheba. She likes to smile. I like her very much.

FOUR

Stupid Boy liked the morning time best. When it was very early and the whole wide world was asleep. He liked it when the sun was out and it all got to be quiet.

His mum and dad lived at the end of a lane. There was a big farm at the other end.

Stupid Boy always waked up early and then he sneaked out of the house and went to watch the farmers. They got out of bed early too. Then they put all the sheep and the cows into new fields.

Stupid Boy got caught.

The End.

The farmers get all the milk and eggs and take it to all the houses. I like to watch when they work very hard with all the farm animals.

One farmer asks me if I want to help. I can collect the eggs from the hens. But I have to be very careful and not drop any and I don't be allowed to make the hens scared. I promise I won't.

I have never picked up chicken eggs before. There are lots of them. I get all the eggs and I give them to the farmer. The farmer says thank you and I go back to the house. I didn't know that Sheba had got out too. I tell Sheba she can be outside. But it is a secret.

Sheba is like Mr. Ted. She is magic and she can read minds too.

STUPID BOY

Me and Sheba go to the pond. I like the pond at the back of the house. There are lots of tadpoles in it. There is a little frog. He still gets his tail. I like to watch him swim. When I throw stones in the water it makes all the baby frogs swim away. They are very fast. Me and Sheba like to watch them. She wags her tail. I don't show Mr. Ted. He doesn't like water. He doesn't be able to swim. But I will tell him all about it. He wishes he can see a frog with a tail.

I don't know Sheba wants to play with the stones. I throw one in the water and then she jumps in and makes a big splash. Then she gets her head under the water and she gets the stone. She gives it back to me. She wags her tail really hard and then she stamps her paws. But I don't want to throw the stone again.

Such a stupid thing for Stupid Boy to do.

I have got Sheba all wet.

I am going to be in big trouble. My dad will send me away on a pirate ship and then I will never get to be seen again. Pirates make people walk the plank. Then they fall in the water and get all eaten by sharks and fishes.

Maybe my dad will send me home to my Nan's house because I got Sheba all wet. Then maybe she will get a cold.

I am bad. Because she is my brother's dog. But my badness got out and Sheba likes to play with me. Maybe on the next weekend they don't want to get me because I am so bad. I always say I am sorry. My mum says I am a liar. But I don't be. I try hard. I am just stupid.

Stupid Boy.

My dad keeps lots of old rags and towels in the shed that is next to the house. I run and get one and then I try to make Sheba all dry again. But her fur is all soaked. I rub her lots of times to make all the water go away, but it doesn't want to.

I get Sheba back in the house. No one has waked up yet. I take Sheba to my den in the basement place where the fridges are. My dad lets me play there. It just has his fridges with lots of dead things in. My dad has lots of dead pigeons and rabbits. He makes pies out of them. They still have all their fur on and there scaredy eyes. Me and Sheba don't look at them. I sit on the floor with my things and play. I have secret food in there and I eat some of it.

My mum and dad don't know about my secret food. Just Mr. Ted and Sheba know about it. I have lots of things in my school bag and then I hide it there and no one finds them. Me and Sheba get to eat chocolate biscuits. But I don't give her lots of them. I have to save them.

My dad wakes up and then he shouts where I am. I keep Sheba in the basement and then I go to the kitchen and tell him I am just playing. He says he is going out all day long and I better be good because he doesn't want to have to deal with me when he gets home. I promise I will. I ask if I can go outside and play with Sheba. He says yes.

STUPID BOY

Me and Sheba play outside all day long. We pretend to be police. She gets to be a police dog and then we look for all the bad people. She likes to play outside. We talk in our heads about it.

My dad doesn't come home until it is nearly dark time. And then me and my brother have to get a bath and go to bed. My dad says he will do it because my mum is tired from keeping care of us all day long. He says he will wash our hair and then put us to bed.

My dad gets my brother bathed and then he tells me to go and get in the water while he puts my brother in bed. My brother gets boats to play with and he left them there. I get to play with them while I wait for my dad to come and wash my hair. But he is getting my brother all dry and then putting him in bed.

My dad gets in the bathroom. He gets the shampoo and then he puts it in my hair and washes it.

"Have you been good today?" he asks me.

I say yes.

"What did you do?"

I tell him about me and Sheba playing police in the lane and looking for bad people. My dad says it is good and he is pleased.

He smiles at me and then I smile all big back at him. I have been good.

My dad gets his hand on my neck and then he press down really hard. It is too fast and I don't know about it. My head gets under the water and I don't be able to get back up because my dad keeps it there and he presses down really hard.

My dad lifts me up again. I don't be able to stop the crying about it and I cough and try to breathe. My dad is smiling. He doesn't have his angry face.

"Do you think I wouldn't know about you sneaking out in the mornings?"

I don't say any words. It is my badness. It always gets the bad things to happen when I don't know it is bad. My dad makes my head squish down in the water again so I don't get to tell him I am sorry about it.

He isn't smiling when he gets me out of the water again. He gets his hands and then he squeezes my chin in his fingers. Maybe he is going to make my mouth fall off. He squeezes it hard. Maybe all my bones will snap.

"If you sneak out again when you are not allowed, maybe next time, I won't let you back up out of the water. Understand?"

I try to make my head nod. But my dad has my chin and he doesn't let it move.

"Get out of the bath and get dressed. Nothing else."

My dad gets to the bedroom too. He takes the bulb out of the lamp.

"Then you can't sneak it on when I go downstairs," he says. "I know what you're like."

I don't mean to be bad all the time. I wished I got to go away. Maybe they can throw me away.

STUPID BOY

Bad Stupid Boy. I make everything bad. All the time.

I get dressed. But I don't get in my bed. He didn't tell me to do that. I stand in the corner and I don't move. Not even a little bit. Maybe he will know about it if I do. I stand in the corner nearly all night long. Then it is my dad's bedtime and I hear his feet when he walks up the stairs.

My dad doesn't talk to me. He gets his clothes off and gets into his bed. I stand there and I don't be able to stop shaking. I get scared in my tummy. Maybe my dad will send me away.

My dad makes a cough noise. I look at him. He smiles and I get in my mum's side of the bed. He doesn't shout at me for not staying in the corner.

My dad gets my hand and then he puts it on his thing. But he doesn't keep it there. Maybe he is going to take my pyjamas off. But he doesn't. He gets my neck like he did at the bath time and then he pushes my head down to put his thing in my mouth.

It gets to the yucky part and then my dad gets my head up and he holds my chin again. He stares at me. But not with his angry eyes. I don't be able to make my mouth swallow. But I try and then it makes the sick want to come out.

"Don't you dare throw up," he says.

I go and get on my sun chair and lie down. I don't hug Mr. Ted.

FIVE

One day, Stupid Boy went for a walk along the river with his dad and Sheba. It was a nice sunny day.

Stupid Boy's dad said, "Don't go on the sand, it makes you sink and don't let Sheba on it."

Stupid Boy stared at the sand. Magic sand that ate you all up. Maybe there got to be a magic place under it with all the sand people inside. Maybe it wasn't so bad to get eaten up by all the sand.

The End.

I don't want Sheba to go and live with the sand people. I keep her close and we run up and down in all the long grass.

Sheba finds a sheep. It is a dead sheep. It lied on its side and has its eyes all open. I poke it with a stick. Sheba thinks it is a good idea to tell my dad.

My dad looks at the sheep.

"Ah yes," he says. "Trolls."

"Trolls?" I ask.

I don't like trolls. Maybe it is them that lives under the sand.

Maybe they will come and get me because I am so stupid and then they will steal me and hide me under the sand forever and ever.

I tell Sheba we are never going to the river ever again. I don't want the trolls to eat her.

STUPID BOY

Me and Sheba tell Mr. Ted about the sheep and the trolls. We tell him that we will never go there again and then the trolls will leave us alone. Me and Mr. Ted draw a picture of the trolls. Maybe they look like monsters with lots of big green hair.

It is time to go home to my Nan's house. My dad has to drive the car over the big bridge that goes over the river. Me and Mr. Ted look out of the window. Maybe we can see the trolls. But it is dark time and I don't be able to see anything. Sheba tries to see them too. But she doesn't see any.

We don't see any trolls all the way to my Nan's house. It is just dark time and people are all getting ready for bed and things. I get scared in my tummy when we get to the road that I live on. I look at my bedroom window. But it makes me all scared when I do that. Maybe the bad man is in there and he can see me. Maybe he is waiting. Mr. Ted thinks he is too. We can feel it all inside. It makes me want to go to the toilet. Mr. Ted is scared too.

My dad takes me in the house. My Nan is sitting in her big chair. She is watching the television. My dad says hello to her and that he will see her next Friday when he picks me up again.

Me and Mr. Ted stand still. Maybe my dad will give me a hug and say bye. But he doesn't. I squeeze Mr. Ted tight. Maybe my dad will miss me when he goes away. My Nan gets up to lock the front door. Me and Mr. Ted go too. We stand at the door and then watch my dad get in the car. We wave at him. But he doesn't wave back at us. Maybe Stupid Boy has been too bad and he doesn't like us at all.

My dad's car goes down the road. I see the red lights at the back go all the way down the dark road. They are like big red monster eyes. I hug Mr. Ted all tight and don't let my breath in. Maybe my dad will come back. Maybe I have been a good boy this time.

My Nan puts her hand on my shoulder and says it is time to go in. We can have hot chocolate and then bed time because I have school tomorrow.

"And not to forget Peter is coming for dinner," she says.

He is. I don't be able to wait about that. He is going to eat at my house and then we are going to play. I don't ever get friends home for dinner before. But my Nan says that it is good fun and then we can play outside and Peter's mum and dad can come and pick him up.

Mr. Ted doesn't be able to wait. He has the bat things all in his tummy about it. We get to bed. Then he lies there and thinks about it before he falls to sleep.

Me and Peter is all excited at school about it too. Peter tells Kirsty he is coming to my house for dinner. She looks sad about it. I say maybe she can come one day. But her mum and dad don't let her do those things. I gave her my special pencil things to look after at the night time and then she don't be sad. She gives me a little frog. We have to keep care of each other's things. I promise I will. Mr. Ted will help me.

Me and Peter walk all by ourselves to my Nan's house. We walk down the alley way and I don't know that my mum is going to be at the house. Maybe Sheba heard us with her magic. She runs up the alley to me and Peter and then she jumps at us and licks all our hands and faces. Then she does her stamp thing and runs all around us in circles. Peter says she is like a crazy dog and then he laughs about it and then she runs back to my mum.

My mum is standing outside at the front gate with my brother. She is smoking her cigarette. Me and Peter get to the garden. My mum coughs very loud in her throat when I try use the front door. She says no and shakes her head.

"Go around the back and take your bags in," she said.

I don't be allowed to use the front door when my mum is there. Just when my Nan is there.

I tell her I am sorry and we go to the back of the house. But then we go back outside because I want to see Sheba. We play lots of games with Sheba. She is very good at pretend. She likes to run very fast too. Me and Peter play catch and she plays too with us. She jumps so high in the air that maybe she will get in the sky.

When dinner is ready we go inside and sit at the big table and we get ravioli with chips. I make mine all open and then I get all the meat out and eat that. Peter doesn't. He just eats his. But he eats it all slow. I make mine go very fast. It is very nice. My brother doesn't eat any dinner with us. He has his baby bottle still. He sits on the floor. He has a new toy. My mum says it is because he is such a good boy that he gets new toys. I try to be good. But I don't be able to keep my badness away. I wish I have toys like my brother.

He always gets all the good toys. My brain tries to call him names. But I want it to shut up because then the bad man will know that I have bad thoughts. Then he will have to come and hurt me because I am bad.

My dad comes and then Peter's mum comes too. She is so big. Bigger than my Nan and my Nan is like giant. Peter's mum has big red hair and she is called Kay. Maybe it is like fire. But she is very nice. She always gives me lots of big smiles about things.

She says hello to my dad and then she asks him if I want to go to dinner at Peter's house in the school holidays. That is the week after. We get a week off school before the summer time. I squeeze myself tight and say please, please in my brain to my dad.

Maybe he can hear me too because he says that I can. Then he asks Kay if maybe Peter wants to come on Friday and sleep over at the weekend. Then maybe he will drop us off at Peter's house when he goes to work on Monday and can pick me up after and Peter if he wants to come too. She says yes.

I am going to get a real sleep over. It is just like magic.

SIX

Stupid Boy was very excited. He feeled it in his tummy. He feeled it in his head. He feeled it everywhere. He got to have his best friend in the whole wide world have a sleepover at his house. He wished he got to tell everyone at school and then he did all the things they did and they didn't get to laugh at Stupid Boy.

The End

Me and Peter talk about the sleepover all the way to the house. We talk about the jungle and the lions and I tell Peter all about the trolls.

My dad says there are bats that get to live in the roof. They live in the roof where I have all my things. Bats are smelly. But trolls like to eat them all up. He says that they are crunchy and then at night time when it all gets dark if me and Peter listen very good. We will be able to hear all the bones being munched up.

Crunch. Crunch. Chomp.

Me and Peter are going to sleep in the big bedroom that is next to my mum and dad's room. We don't get a bed. But there is a tent thing that looks like a truck.

I am so stupid though. I don't know about the monster that comes. The jungle doesn't keep him away. The big monster gets in the truck and then he gets me and squishes me all dead. Because the truck is a spooky truck where all the bad things get to happen. I don't tell Mr. Ted about it or Peter.

My dad has got the truck all made. It is made of white poles and then it has a truck cover. Me and Peter say it is a super truck. It can drive on the water and then it doesn't sink. And we can live in the jungle and drive over all the crocodiles.

Me and Peter get lots of papers and then we put them all over the floor. We have to stand on the paper. Because if our feet get in the water then we fall in and die and no one ever comes to help us. Even if we scream lots of loud all the time.

Peter says maybe we can get to play hide and seek. He says the house is all big and I will never ever find him because it has lots of rooms and then it even has two lots of stairs. We ask my dad. Maybe he will say no. He doesn't like stupid games. Only Stupid Boy plays stupid games.

My dad says that we don't be able to make lots of noise. My mum doesn't feel very well and she is watching the television with my brother. My dad is making dinner. He makes nice dinners. I get to eat dinner when Peter is there because my badness doesn't come out and make everything wrong when I don't know about it.

I don't take the medicine too. Maybe my mum doesn't like it any more. She just does it sometimes. But not all the time. Maybe she doesn't be very good at remembering to do it.

Me and Peter have lots of fun and we hide in lots of places. Peter doesn't be very good at the hiding part. He doesn't be able to hide from the clock monster that makes growl noises. Then he says tick tock and is going to eat Peter all up. He scares Peter from where he gets to hide.

I like being the clock monster. Me and Mr. Ted have made a story about him. Clock monster eats children when they are late for things.

Peter runs and hides again. He hides in lots of places. He even hides in the kitchen with my dad. There is big stairs there and Peter hides under them. My dad says he can and then he doesn't tell me where Peter is.

I look lots of times. But I don't see Peter. I make clock monster noises. But then my dad makes them too and he is a clock monster and he is going to get me and eat me all up. He says he will. He makes lots of growl noises and then he is too fast for me and he gets me in his big arms and makes me not stop laughing because I am ticklish.

I yell lots and shout Peter so that he can come and save me. Peter gets out from his hiding place and then we try to get my dad's arms open. But he is too strong. My dad falls over and then we get away. We don't be able to stop the laughing. We run up the stairs to get away from the clock monster. He is going to get us again.

I run faster than Peter. I get up the stairs to the top before he does. My dad is coming. I shout at Peter to run away. Peter doesn't be able to and then my dad catches him and Peter laughs lots because my dad tickles him too much.

STUPID BOY

My dad pulls Peter's pants down and I laugh for Peter to get away. My dad laughs about it too. But my dad gets Peter's leg and I am scared in my tummy. My dad might do the hurt thing to him because we are too loud and then it is my fault because it is my badness, not Peter's. It is me who is bad. Peter doesn't have any badness inside him. My mum says he is retarded because he is a little slow from bad things that made him sick when he was a baby. But he doesn't be bad. Peter is nice.

I get Peter and then I don't want to play hide and seek anymore. It is nearly dinner time anyway. Then I have to get a bath. But it doesn't matter. My mum says Peter can play with my brother in the lounge. I go to the bath first because Peter is there and then my mum says she wants us to be upstairs and not in the way.

My dad says my brother can use the water after me and that I can make the bath. I don't know how to do it. My dad says he will show me.

We go to the bathroom and then my dad puts the hot tap on. He makes the bubbles from my brother's special bottle and then he pours some of the stuff in. He says that I have to swish it all about with my hands. And then it makes all the bubbles inside. It does. I am going to tell Mr. Ted about it. We don't know that making a hand swish makes all the bubbles.

My dad asks me if me and Peter is having lots of fun and I say we are. I tell him about the truck that can swim on the water. He thinks that it is a good idea.

"Make the bubbles big with your hand," he says.

The water is hot. My dad pulls my pants off. I swish the hot water lots and then my dad asks what we are going to do when we go to bed and maybe we would like to take some food with us.

My dad makes his thing to do the hurt thing and then I put both my hands in the water to make lots and lots of bubbles. They are going to be the biggest bubbles in the world. The water is very hot. It makes my hands all pink. I don't talk to my dad about the hurt thing he gets to do. Then he will know my badness is there and he will make it hurt lots more.

My dad makes all his funny noises like the clock monster. He puts his pants back up and tells me to get some cold water in it. Then to get in the bath and he will come back and get my hair washed. I tell him okay.

I let my eyes cry in the bath. Then no one can see it.

Stupid Boy is too bad inside.

STUPID BOY

SEVEN

Stupid Boy got to have dinner at his friend's house. He got to eat it all up until he was very fat. Stupid Boy and his friend got to play outside. They played on roller skates and had races. They played tag. Stupid Boy got to be the one that was tagging everyone lots of times. He got to laugh a lot.

Stupid Boy liked to laugh.

He felt sad when it was time to go home. His friend's mum took him in her big white car to his dad's work.

When Stupid Boy got to his dad's work place. His dad had a big surprise.

The End

I am very excited. I stand there and smile very big. I don't know what it is that my dad has got for a surprise.

My dad pulls out the biggest bike in the whole world. My dad has got me a big bike. It is yellow and has a seat with a back on it. It has gears too. Three gears. Not four. Four is bad. But it is just three and it can go fast. It is called a Chopper. I like it very much. My dad says that someone was going to put it in the tip, but then he says he would have it because it just needed to have a new wheel. My dad got a new wheel and he put it on. I am very lucky. The bike is all mine.

J D STOCKHOLM

We put the bike in the car and take it home. I can't wait to show Sheba. Then we can play outside. But we will keep away from the trolls.

Trolls will steal the bike and then take it away into the sand and I won't have it anymore.

I tell my dad thank you and then I promise to look after the bike forever.

My dad says I can keep it in the room next to the front door. We don't use it because the room is all messy. My mum and dad just have lots of boxes in there and my new bike. I show it to Sheba and Mr. Ted. They like it very much too. Me and Sheba get to play out lots on the bike. She runs with me. She runs very fast.

Every day we play with it.

It is too cold in the morning. It is near the weekend. I get the bike and then I lean it against the door so I can get my coat on. My brother is here. He doesn't get a bike because he is just too little. But he likes mine and he makes the peddles move. But the bike falls over and it hits the door. The door is big and made of glass and the bike falls through it.

I am scared in my tummy because the glass is all broken and it falls on the floor. I make my brother move. And he cries about it. My mum comes. She asks what has happened and I tell her my bike fell over. She is going to get mad and shout at me. But she doesn't shout and she doesn't say any bad words.

"Who did it?" she asks.

STUPID BOY

I don't want to get my brother in big trouble because then maybe my dad will do the hurt thing to him and he will cry too much. I tell my mum I knocked it over on accident.

"You should go and play outside," she says. "I have to clear all the glass."

I don't want her to make her hands cut. Maybe the glass will get them all chopped off and then there will be blood all over the floor and she will die. I tell my mum I will help. But she says no thank you.

I play on my bike all day long. I ride down all the lanes. I don't go to where the trolls are though. I don't want them to get my bike. Maybe they will take it and keep it in the sand. Sheba plays with me. We play outside until it is nearly dark time.

I have to take my bike all around the back of the house. I don't like it very much because it is dark and the garden is all big and giant. It has giant grass too and maybe the trolls get to hide in there. I have to get my bike on the little bridge thing so it doesn't get wet from the water that goes to the pond.

I don't know that my dad is in his garage thing in the garden. He keeps his bike in there and lots of junk, my mum says. I don't see the light is on. I get to the back door to take my bike in. I hear a big noise. It is my dad. He runs from the garage to me and then he hits me in the face and I fall over and bang myself on the wall. I cry. My dad picks me up and takes me inside. He shouts for my mum.

"Stop crying," he shouts at me.

He shouts at me about the glass and the door. He asks me why I made it all broken. My mum comes and then she tells him that she has cleaned it all up and that my brother didn't get hurt by it. My dad puts his face in mine.

"You are very lucky," he says. "I don't have the money to get the door fixed. What would you have done if your brother had fallen and cut himself?"

I don't say any words. I keep crying and my dad gets mad about that. He doesn't like it when I cry. I am a big fat stupid baby. Big fat Stupid Boy. My dad asks me what happened. I shrug my shoulders.

"You better give me an answer."

"I dropped my bike and it made the glass smash," I say.

My dad gets his hand and then he hits me across the face. My brother starts to cry too.

"Are you happy now?"

I make the whole house upset. He tells me to go and sit on the chair and shut up. He says I have to think about what he should do to teach me a lesson because he has got me a new bike and I couldn't be good even with that.

My dad tells me to sit on the chair at the dinner table. He says I get to sit there and think about everything and when I have a good answer at what he should do then I have to tell him. He leans over and then he whispers at me.

STUPID BOY

"You can sit there forever."

I sit on my hands. I watch my feet. They swing. I wish Mr. Ted is with me or Sheba. But my dad makes Sheba go away and Mr. Ted is upstairs in bed. I sit on the chair forever.

It gets to supper time. My mum likes supper at night time. My dad tells me to make the table nice for my mum and him. He tells me to do it properly and if I don't then there will be lots more trouble for me. He makes my tummy all scared inside. It jumps up and down and it makes me need to go to the toilet. I don't be able to though. I don't want to ask my dad. He will be mad and say no.

My dad stands there and he does the stare thing. He asks if I have thought about my lesson and what it is going to be. I shake my head. I don't know. My dad comes to the table to see what I am doing. He sits in the chair where I am making it nice. My hands shake because maybe he is going to hit me like on surprise and I won't know about it. I don't want to look at him because he is there and he is smiling. I feel all bad inside. I wish I can tell my dad I am sorry about the glass.

My dad tells me to go and sit back on my chair. I get the chair at the other side of the table. It is near the back door. It is cold sitting there. I don't be able to stop the shivers. Maybe the bad man will come because I am very bad. He doesn't ever come to my mum and dad's house before. I always try to be on my bestest behaviour there and then Mr. Ted can tell the bad man I am good.

My mum and dad eat their supper. They sit at the table too. My dad tells my mum that I am so bad he is making me think about how I should learn my lesson. My mum says it is a good idea. She doesn't know what to do with me anymore. I am just bad all the time.

She can't wait for Sunday then I can go home to my Nan and then I am her problem.

I don't let my eyes cry about it.

My mum says, "I wish I never had bloody kids."

She hates them.

My dad tells me that I have to get all the plates and things away at the sink so then my mum can get them clean. He stands and watches me get all the things off the table. He leans on the side. He makes his arms folded and I go past him to get all the things in the sink. I squeeze myself all tight. Maybe he will hit me because I don't know my answer yet. He does the stare thing again. I don't like to look at his face when he does that. It makes me more scared in my tummy.

My brain keeps having pictures about my dad. It wants to show me that my dad is going to jump out and then he will hit me very hard and do the hurt thing because I am so bad.

My dad tells me to go to bed.

EIGHT

Stupid Boy got a new friend. His friend was very nice. He was called Andrew. Stupid Boy and Andrew got to play together all the time. Stupid Boy was very lucky to have a friend like Andrew. Andrew was very special.

He played with Stupid Boy all the time.

He didn't get mad when Stupid Boy didn't be able to ride on bikes.

He didn't tell Stupid Boy to go away when he was in a bad mood.

He didn't tell Stupid Boy he was a baby when he got to cry.

Andrew was invisible.

The End

Mr. Ted and Sheba like Andrew. They play with him too and Andrew likes Sheba and Mr. Ted. He thinks they are very special.

Andrew likes to play games. We play police and Sheba is the police dog. We play monster hunters and Sheba is the magic talking dog and we play pirates and Mr. Ted is the parrot and Sheba is the pirate dog. Me and Andrew like to play pretend all the time.

When I get scared and sad in my tummy I get my eyes closed and then I think about all the games I play with Andrew. They make me very happy to think about. I tell Andrew all my secret things and Andrew doesn't ever be mad about it. He doesn't think I am horrible and yucky and smelly or stupid.

Andrew is my best friend.

I lie in my bed all night long and cry because I have been bad and smashed the door. Andrew sits on the floor and we make up stories in our brains so we don't talk and make noise. It makes me feel better. Maybe in the light time we can make an adventure.

My mum and dad don't see Andrew sit on the floor when it is their bedtime. Andrew is invisible.

My best friend in the whole wide world.

I lie in bed all night long. I don't move. Not at all. Like a lie down statue. I am good at being a statue. I don't ever move. Maybe not even breathe. Mr. Ted is good too. He doesn't move. I don't even wipe my eyes or my nose when they are all wet and snotty and they make my face feel funny.

It is my mum and dad's bedtime. I only move my eyes and then they think I am asleep. Then they don't be mad at me for being awake when it is late at night.

I don't be able to sleep. I am too scared about it. My eyes try lots of times. Then I make them wake up again and open. Maybe my dad will drag me out of bed because I took too long to decide about the lesson. Or maybe the bad man will come and no one will know about it because they are all asleep. Maybe my mum and dad will take me back to my Nan's house and then they will never want to see me again because my mum wishes she doesn't get any bloody kids.

I wish I can be good and then she will like me and she won't hate me and my brother because he doesn't be bad. He doesn't have any badness inside. It is just me. I am the bad one.

Me, me, me. Forever.

I try to be quiet and I get Mr. Ted and then I put him on my eyes and squeeze him all tight so the tears don't come out anymore. They make my head hurt. Maybe it will pop open. Mr. Ted hugs my head very hard to keep the stupid crying away. I wish I can get up and then I can go and play with Andrew and not be the stupid boy who cries.

My eyes want to fall asleep and they keep doing it. Andrew sits on the floor next to the bed so he can talk to me in my brain. Mr. Ted lets me hug him all up to keep all the badness away and Sheba sleeps on the floor by the door. Then the bad man doesn't get in. Maybe if they know about my badness they wouldn't like me too and then they will go away and leave me behind.

It's morning time. I am awake and my mum and dad are still asleep. I don't get out of bed. I don't know if I am allowed to. My tummy hurts because I didn't go to the toilet yet and I am all bursting. But I don't be able to let it out because I will be in very big trouble. I don't want to go because then I have to ask my dad and he will be mad at me about it. He will be mad that I talk to him.

My mum and dad wake up. It is Saturday. My dad doesn't have to go to work. But he makes bacon for my mum on Saturdays. He gets out of bed and tells me to get dressed and then he tells me to come downstairs and get the table ready. My mum has her cigarette and then she gets my brother out of his bed.

I ask my mum if I can go to the toilet. She nods her head. I go there as fast as I can. Then I don't get in trouble for taking lots of time. I go back to the bedroom. I make my bed all nice and tidy and get it all the same so it doesn't get any lines in it. I put my pyjamas and I fold them all up and put them right in the middle so they are in the right place and I don't get told off. Then I get my slippers and I put them with the other shoes and I make them in a nice neat line. My mum doesn't get mad at me when everything is in the right place. Mr. Ted thinks it is good.

I go in the kitchen and then I make that all nice and tidy too. My dad tells me to sit on the chair again. He asks me if I have decided about the lesson. I shake my head. I don't look at him. I look at my feet and then I sit on the chair and not move at all.

My dad gets a bowl of cornflakes and then he puts it on the table in front of me. He sits down in the chair that is next to me. He tells me to eat it. It is for me. I tell my dad thank you. I don't feel hungry in my tummy. But I get the bowl and then I get the cornflakes and put some in my mouth. My mouth doesn't want to chew it all up.

I don't be able to stop the crying from coming. It makes me not be able to eat my cereal because my mouth wants to cry and then my throat doesn't want to swallow it. Maybe I will get the sick out of my tummy. My dad does the stare thing. But he doesn't have his angry face. He just stares at me. I don't want to look at him because he is too mad at me for the glass. I am just so bad. Maybe they will send me away forever. I don't ever be good. My dad tells me to stop the crying. I try to make it go away. I nod my head and squeeze it all away.

I sit on the chair all day long. My legs get tired and then they feel like they are invisible. I shiver because it is cold by the door. My dad says I can only move when I set the table. Then I am allowed to go to the bathroom too.

My dad has a study upstairs. He sits there and reads or draws or does some work things. I don't know if I am allowed to get off the chair. But my dad says when I have decided I have to find him and tell him. I am scared in my tummy when I go up the stairs. Maybe he will be mad at me. But I get up there and then I knock on the door and he tells me to come in.

I tell him that I have an answer. He says that's good and tells me to wait until he is finished reading. I stand there a long time. I don't move. My legs are sore and I try to let my feet move a little bit. My dad tells me to stand still because I am making him not be able to read his book. I look at the clock my dad has. It is on top of the fireplace. My mum got it for his birthday. It has spinning balls at the bottom and is all gold. The little hand is at the eight and then it is on the nine. It goes nearly all the way to ten. Then my dad finishes his book and he puts it down and says it is bedtime.

I ask my dad if we can read a book at bedtime. Maybe I can tell him I am sorry. I squeeze myself all tight because maybe he will want to shout at me about asking. But he says yes and it is a good idea. He tells me to go and get my pyjamas on and then get in the big bed.

I do what I am told. I get in the bed. I take Mr. Ted too. I hug him all tight. I lie there and then my dad comes and he gets in bed too. I tell my dad I am sorry for the glass door. I tell him it is on accident and I don't mean it. I say I won't ever do it again. I don't be able to stop the crying again. I always cry like a big fat stupid baby.

I try to hug my dad too. He lets me lie on his arm. I hug him lots. Me and Mr. Ted do it. Then my dad tells me to turn around and he tells me I don't need to cry about it. He gets the book and starts to read it and I don't move his hand when he gets my pants off. My dad does the hurt thing. I hug Mr. Ted very tight and I am like Andrew. I am invisible and then we play.

NINE

Stupid Boy is so bad his mum and dad don't want him anymore. He broke the glass and makes everyone mad. He is stupid and bad. They take him back home and throw him away.

The End

I am a stupid boy and I fall to sleep.
I don't hear the man. I let him creep.
Maybe it is the bad man. Maybe the bad man comes because of the glass.
It is a different man. Maybe a new bad man.
The man shakes me and shakes me until my head nearly falls off. I shout my loudest. As big as I can. I scream and I shout. Maybe I huff and I puff. But the man is there and he has got in and I didn't hear him because I was asleep and now the man is going to get me and hurt me and then chop me into a million pieces.
My Nan is gone. I don't know where. I didn't see her get away. Maybe it is magic and the man makes her invisible.
No one is going to save me.
I cry.
I don't know that the man has got in the bedroom. I was asleep. I didn't hear him and I didn't hear my Nan get out of bed. I don't know where she is. I shout very loud. I scream and close my eyes and try to make him all go away. But he

doesn't and maybe he is like the bad man. Maybe he is going to scratch and bite me and then do the hurt thing and hit me when I cry. Because I am stupid. I am Stupid Boy. Maybe he is a new bad man.

I get Mr. Ted and I try to get off the bed. But the man stands there and he says my name. He says it lots of times. But in my tummy I want to run away. I shout very loud for my Nan. I don't be able to get my screams all out.

The man doesn't shout at me and then he doesn't try and get me and do any hurt things. He stands up and then he says he is the ambulance man and it is okay. He says my Nan is downstairs. I stop all the shouting at him. I stand at the window. Me and Mr. Ted stand there. Maybe the man will still come and get us.

He asks me if I have shoes and a coat. I nod my hardest. Hard enough to make my head fall off. But it doesn't. I wish I have Sheba and Andrew with me and then they will know what to do. I make the breathing feel scratchy in my nose. I make it do it one, two, three times. Then I start again.

The man asks me where they are. I say they are downstairs. I make the D and the T in my mouth. But I say it again because I have to make it the same. I feel the D and the T again. Downstairs I say it again. But that is two and I say it three times. But three times wasn't the same. It doesn't be equal. Four is bad. Five is like three. I say the word downstairs six times.

STUPID BOY

Six D's and six T's. The man still stands there. He doesn't go away. I forgot he is standing there. He goes in the hall but he doesn't go away. He tells me it is okay and we should get my coat. I don't want him to say the downstairs word.

"You can get a ride in the ambulance," he says.

I don't ever do that before. I have a toy ambulance. I have got it off Graham. It is all metal and shiny. But I don't ever see inside a real one. I am excited in my tummy about it and then I follow the ambulance man.

I tell Mr. Ted we can because the ambulance man says so. But I don't say the words with my mouth. Mr. Ted can read minds too. So he knows what I say to him about it. He is excited too. I know he smiles at me about it and he thinks it is okay to go downstairs. We walk very carefully. I don't get the side of the carpet to feel through my shoes. But when we get on the stairs. We have to get the edge in the middle of our feet. Then nothing bad will happen.

My Nan is at the bottom of the stairs. She is in a special chair and she has a blanket and I want to run down. But I don't be able to because then maybe I get the numbers wrong.

I count.

One, two, three and then I do it again and again until we get to the bottom.

I do it all the way down. Not four. Four is bad. If I make it four then the bad man will come and maybe my Nan will go to heaven and I don't want her to go there. I don't get to go and see my Gaga there. I don't want to be sad because my Nan is in heaven.

My Nan is crying. She tells me she is sorry. But she doesn't have to be sorry. She doesn't be bad. I am bad. All the time. Maybe she needs an ambulance because of my badness. I am bad. That is why my dad takes me back to my Nan's early. My Nan doesn't be able to give me lots of hugs back. She has a needle thing in her hand and then she has something on her other arm and then the ambulance man is squeezing a thing and making it all hiss.

The ambulance man gets my Nan in the ambulance and the other man gets my Nan's keys and then they lock the door. But no one checks that it is locked. My brain gets the pictures about the bad man and maybe he will get in because the door doesn't be locked properly. I don't look at my window upstairs. Maybe he is there already and I don't know about it. Maybe he looks out the window and then he smiles at me.

I tell Mr. Ted the door is locked. I saw the ambulance man do it. I wish I can go and check it. But I don't be able to so I do the stare thing at it. Maybe no one will get in when we go in the ambulance.

We get to the hospital and my Nan sits in a chair because we are waiting for her doctor and then me and Mr. Ted sit in another one. My legs keep doing the fast shake thing. My mum doesn't like when I do that. She says I am something called a fidget. She always tells me to keep still. But it keeps my badness away and then my brain doesn't get all the bad pictures in it. I squeeze Mr. Ted all tight. I keep talking to my Nan. My mouth doesn't want to shut up. But she is all tired and she keeps getting her eyes closed. She says she is resting them. But she doesn't talk to me when I talk. Maybe she falls asleep.

My dad comes to the hospital. But he doesn't ride in an ambulance. He drives his car. I hear his voice when he talks to the nurse outside. He has his mad voice on. I tell Mr. Ted that I am sorry. I don't know I have done anything bad. Maybe I do it and I don't notice. Maybe my dad is still all mad about the glass. Because he makes me go home the next day. Then they all went out on the Monday and don't take me because I am bad.

My dad tells me to come on and follow him to the car. I do. I get behind him and I hug Mr. Ted and then we walk through the hospital. My dad walks very fast. Me and Mr. Ted run behind him. It is dark time outside and we get in the car and drive all the way home. My dad says bad things about my Nan. He uses all the bad words and says she is selfish. I don't think she is selfish. She is nice.

I feel all sad inside. I tell Mr. Ted to please not let my Nan go to heaven.

TEN

The bell had already made its noise at Stupid Boy's school. He was late. Late boys got eaten by monsters. Everyone knew that.

Stupid Boy got to his classroom and all the children stared at him. Stupid Boy was stupid for being so late. The teacher asked him where he had been and he didn't know. He said he was sorry.

The teacher was mad.

"It isn't good manners to be late," she said to him.

Stupid Boy feeled bad inside. He said he was sorry again.

His teacher said he had to take a note to the office. The teacher gave Stupid Boy the note to add his name to the register. Maybe they would put it in big fat red letters.

STUPID BOY WAS STUPID AND LATE.

The End.

I take the note to the office. The office lady has an angry face. She doesn't like me. No one likes Stupid Boy.

The office lady tells me that I am in big trouble. She opens the big giant doors and then she tells me to come inside.

She makes me go down the stairs. Maybe it is a dungeon down there. Where they put children to forget about them and then the rats eat them all up and get to be big fat rats.

Maybe the office lady will lock Stupid Boy in the dungeon.

Forever.

My dad doesn't talk to me when we get in the house. I get inside and then me and Mr. Ted get upstairs. Sheba is there and she wags her tail very hard and stamps her paws. I don't stroke her head. My dad will be mad about it. But then Sheba wants to bark about it. Because she can talk.

My dad tells her to shut up and he might make her go downstairs if she gets to bark some more. She nearly makes me fall over on the floor. She gets to rub on my legs. I touch her head and tell her I don't be allowed to. I hope she can hear me in her brain about it.

I get in my bed at the bottom of my mum and dad's bed. Then I lie there and hug Mr. Ted. It is all cold in my bed. I squeeze my legs up and close my eyes. I hope my Nan is okay all alone. Maybe she is still asleep. I hope I get to see her tomorrow.

Me and Mr. Ted wake up before everyone when it gets to light time. Even my brother gets to still be sleeping. We don't get out of bed though. That will get me in lots of big trouble and I don't want my mum and dad to get mad at me again. I lie there and wait for them to get up. It gets to eight and then the alarm wakes them all up.

My mum and dad get out of bed. I don't move. I don't know if I get to be allowed to yet and

I don't want to make my mum and dad shout at me about it. I get to be good at not moving. I don't move at all. Maybe I am a good dead body. Maybe my mum and dad will think I am dead and then I get to go to heaven.

My mum gets her cigarette.

"Get out of bed and get ready for school," she says.

But I don't have my uniform there. I just get my pyjamas and my shoes and my coat because I didn't know I was going to get a sleep over at my mum and dad's house.

I tell my mum I don't have any uniform. My dad gets to swear about it. He doesn't like to always have to run around for me.

"You are nothing but a drain on my life," he says.

I don't mean to be. I am sorry. He gets his angry eyes and then he does the stare thing at me.

I sit on my bed. I make it all nice and tidy and I get all the corners right. Just three of them. I make number four different. Mr. Ted sits on my knee and I look down at his head. I don't want to see my dad's face because he will shout at me. Maybe I can make myself all small and then invisible and I can go away forever then I don't be a pain for my dad.

My mum and dad get my brother and then they all go downstairs. My dad doesn't tell me if I can go too. I ask Mr. Ted but he doesn't know. And then Sheba gets up and she goes downstairs.

Maybe she is telling me what to do. So I go there too. Like Sheba.

I sit at the kitchen table. It is all big and giant. Andrew gets to sit there too. He doesn't say anything. He does the same as me and then we both sit and be quiet. Maybe me and Andrew can play outside later. When I get to finish school. I hug Mr. Ted under the table. Maybe he doesn't be allowed to be there.

My mum and dad and my brother all sit at the table. My mum and dad eat some bacon and some eggs. My brother gets his baby bottle. He never likes to eat food. Unless it is crisps and chocolate. He likes those.

My mum says that she didn't know I was coming to stay at the house so they don't have anything to give me for breakfast. Because it is all still at my Nan's house. I say it is okay. I don't really be hungry anyway.

I watch the clock instead. My school time has started. I am going to be late. Then I will have to walk in and all the other children will do the stare thing at me. Then I will have to take a late note to the office and the mean office lady will do her angry face and be mad at me about it.

My mum and dad eat all their breakfast and then they go and get dressed. I stay in the kitchen and then Sheba comes in because it is her breakfast time too. When my dad isn't looking at me. I stroke her head. She smiles at me.

My dad takes us all to my Nan's house. I am very late for school. The little hand is nearly at the ten. All the other children will be there and they will have got the register done and then maybe I will miss my milk in the morning.

"Go upstairs and get your uniform on," my mum says.

But I don't want to go alone. Maybe the bad man is there because the ambulance man didn't check the door and then maybe the bad man got in. Me and Mr. Ted walk up slow. I count. It keeps the pictures of the bad man away. I make the click noise so it gets to scratch my throat and keep all the bad things away.

My dad tells me to hurry up and get upstairs or he will drag me there himself. I don't want him to drag me upstairs. Maybe he will do the hurt thing because I am bad. Sheba wants to come. But she doesn't be allowed to. I can only take Mr. Ted. Me and Mr. Ted get up there slowly and we listen all the way when we count. The bad man isn't there. But maybe my heart wants to go pop inside because it gets all scared.

I get my uniform all on and then I run down the stairs. I say bye to my mum and then I run my fastest all the way to school. I am very late. It is passed the ten. All the children are on their break time. Kirsty and Peter are there in the playground. They ask me where I have been. I don't want to tell them. Then they will think my Nan is bad and say bad words about her like my mum and dad do.

STUPID BOY

I go to the office. I don't like the lady. She has big glasses and they look funny on her nose. She always likes to shout at people. She asks why I am late. I tell her it is because we don't leave the house for a long time. She says if I am late again she will call my dad.

I tell her I am sorry.

ELEVEN

When Stupid Boy got all growed up he was going to be a knight. He would have a big giant helmet and a sword. It was going to be a magic sword. He would have a big shield and it would have a big red lion on it.

Stupid Boy and Andrew played knights. They were secret knights.

Stupid Boy took the late slip to the mean office lady. She got mad and she shouted and smoke got out of her nose.

She got Stupid Boy and throwed him in the dungeon.

The End.

My Nan is poorly and she has to stay at the hospital so they can make her all better again. She wants to go and see my Gaga because she is sad and misses him. But she doesn't be able to go to heaven. She took lots of magic medicine to make her fall to sleep and go to see him. But she got scared and then she didn't go and the ambulance man came. My Nan says she is sorry. She won't do it again. I tell her it is okay. I give her a big hug about it. She doesn't be bad.

My mum says my Nan is just sick in the head.

STUPID BOY

"Maybe it would be good if she just died and then we wouldn't have to deal with all this crap," she says.

I don't want my Nan to die. Maybe the hospital will make her feel better. She says she has some medicine to make her feel happy.

We see my Nan at dinner time when my dad has finished from work. Then we get to go to the hospital. I don't be allowed to stay in there. There are lots of poorly people and my mum says I make too much noise. So me and Sheba get to play outside in the grass and the trees. We play with Andrew and then we get to be knights like in my brother's cartoon about it.

My mum lets me take my skates. They are really good to skate there because I skate in the car park. The road part is all nice and very good for my skates. I go fast. They don't be new skates. My Nan got them at a flea market. She doesn't be able to buy new ones. But I like them. They are black with orange wheels and I can skate fast in them.

My Nan lets me take them when I go to Peter's house too. We skate on his road. But I don't go to Peter's house now because my Nan is poorly in the hospital. Then I don't like when he comes to my mum and dad's house. He is my friend and maybe my dad thinks he is bad too and then he tries to do the hurt thing to him. Peter doesn't be bad.

I sleep at my mum and dad's all the time. I don't be allowed to stay at my Nan's because she doesn't be there and I don't get to stay on my own. I wish my mum and dad's house is next to my Nan's house and then I don't be late for school all the time. My dad doesn't go to work until the little hand is at the ten and then I am late and I get in big trouble about it.

My dad drops me at the gate. He drives away to his work. I keep the crying away and walk up the playground. It doesn't be locked all the time. I get the sick feeling in my tummy. Maybe it will want to come out and then I will be in trouble about that. I get to my classroom. I feel all bad inside when I open the door and then the teacher stares at me because I am late again. She gives me a note to take to the office so they can put my name in the register.

The office lady does the mad breathing thing about it.

"What do I have to do to make you be on time?" she asks. "You aren't so special that you get to start at a different time to everyone else."

I don't know. I tell her I don't know.

It gets to Friday and then it is the same. I get late again. I run my fastest when my dad drops me off. But the register has gone to the office and then I get the late slip and have to give it to the office lady. The office lady does the stare thing like my dad and she has angry eyes too. I say I am sorry. I say my dad doesn't work until ten.

The office lady gets out of the office and she stands in front of me. She is big and fat and has a big stupid skirt on. She stands with her hands on her hips and she tells me I am a liar.

I don't be a liar. Not ever.

She bends down and says I am. I don't look at her. I look at my feet. Then I don't have to see her stupid eyes and glasses. I fold my arms and squeeze them all tight. Then I get to keep my mouth closed because I want to say bad things and my badness will come out.

"I have to call your parents over this," she says.

My tummy does the jump thing. I look around because maybe my dad is coming to get me. Maybe I will have to go home again and then I will be in big trouble. He will hit me and shout at me and I am sorry. I am late on accident. I keep the squeezing part then I don't get any cries or any badness. I don't get anything. I make my brain do the counting inside. I count when I squeeze my arms and then I let go again.

She says my dad tells her that I am late because I mess around in the morning. I don't want to go to school and I am bad. I am making my mum sick with it all the time because they don't know what to do about my behaviour.

I tell her I don't be a liar.

"Your mum and dad say you are," she says. "Your dad says you don't behave."

I get my hands in my hair and then I pull it lots of hard and I make it all go away. I don't be a liar. I don't. But I don't get to keep saying it. She tells me to shut up and that I should behave. My dad is a liar not me. But she doesn't believe me.

"Should I call your dad and ask him?"

I make my breathing all scratchy inside. The office lady tells me to go away and on Monday I don't be allowed to be late or I will be in the biggest trouble ever.

STUPID BOY

TWELVE

Stupid Boy got in bed.
Stupid Boy pretended to be dead
Stupid Boy went away
Stupid Boy got to play.

The End.

Me and Andrew and Sheba and Mr. Ted all play. There are some frames at the front of the house. My dad maked them. He put planks on them and ropes and ladders. They are very high and I can climb bigger than the house.

I play on it lots of times.

Sheba doesn't be able to go to the top. She doesn't be able to climb on the ladders. She stays at the bottom and then she is the guard dragon who keeps all the monsters away and when they come she lights them all on fire.

Andrew, Mr. Ted and me all climb to the top and then we sit on the plank. We can see for lots of miles around. We watch for the bad people coming and if they do, I will get my sword and chop off their heads.

There is an evil black cat. He doesn't get a name; he is so bad that no one knows what to call him. He has big, scary, yellow eyes and he makes all the other cats sad. He beats them when they don't do as they are told. He is bad and he is a bully. He is going to make all the other cats into slaves and then kill them and feed them to all the dogs.

I see the evil black cat come to the land. I wave my sword at him and tell him to go away. The black cat tries to be mean. He hisses and gets his claws out. But Andrew is magic and he tells the black cat he will make him into a worm if he doesn't go away.

Andrew starts to say all the magic words. Black cat runs away.

I see the little brown cat. She is called Susie. She is little and brown and all scared in her tummy. She hides from black cat.

I get Susie and hug her lots and tell her black cat will never ever get to come back and be mean to her ever, ever again.

Susie cat is nice. I put her in the cat thing on my tummy and then I carry her all the way to the top. We sit and watch black cat run away.

Sheba the dragon barks at black cat. He is just a scaredy cat.

It is Monday. The office lady says I don't be allowed to be late ever again. I wish I got to take Andrew and Sheba and then they can make the office lady run away like a scaredy cat. Then she doesn't ever come back. I wake up very early. My mum and dad are still in bed and I sit with Mr. Ted and we wait for them to wake up too.

When they do get all waked up, they get my brother up and dressed. Me and Mr. Ted get dressed too and we make sure that everything is right and nice and tidy. I get my uniform on and then my shoes and I don't forget anything at all.

We sit in the kitchen and then we wait for my mum and dad to eat all their breakfast. I watch the clock and it is passed nine again. I don't have Mr. Ted because I left him on the bed. I don't be allowed to take him to school. But I have my bag and I hug that very tight and wish we can go because I don't want to get into lots of trouble for being late again.

I get to school. It is all quiet. The gate has been locked and I have to use the big gate that is at the front that goes to the big doors. It is near the stupid fat office lady with her stupid fat glasses. Maybe she will get to see me and shout. Maybe she will see me be late and maybe she will get to shout at me two times. I don't want her to shout at me anymore. She will call my dad and he will come in and I will get in lots of trouble.

I wish my Nan would get better then I can sleep at her house on school days and I don't be late. But my mum says it will be a long time because she has to talk to the doctor about her head. My mum says my Nan is crazy and they don't want to let her go home again because she misses my Gaga and wants to go to heaven.

Maybe they will lock me up in the hospital too. My mum says I am evil and crazy too. She says I am like my Nan. Maybe they get to know that I miss my Gaga too. But I know I don't be able to go to heaven. He can watch me until I am all grown up. He told me about that part.

I get to my classroom very fast. My teacher gives me the register and then she gives me a late slip too. She tells me that I might as well take the book because I have to go to the office anyway. I do what I am told. I walk down the long hall to the office. I open the register book and I look at my name. It has an 'O' by it, but because I am late the office lady will have to change it to an 'L'. I get my pencil and then I change it so it is the same as all the others. It gets a line and then it doesn't say I am late.

Maybe the office lady will know about it. I give her the register book. But I keep my late slip in my pocket. I don't look at her with her stupid glasses. Maybe she will know what I did and then I will get a big shouting at. She asks me if I was late today and I shrug my shoulders and look at my feet. She gets the register open. I can feel all the scared in my tummy feeling. Maybe she will stand up and come and shout at me.

I get the scratchy feeling in my nose when I get to breathe. I do it six times. Six is good and then the office lady won't know about the book and that I changed it. Six is like magic. It doesn't let me be in trouble about things. The office lady doesn't say any more things to me.

I get to go to the toilet. I feel all bad in my tummy. Maybe someone will know what I did. Maybe the office lady will look at it when I am not there and then she will know that I am bad really because I changed it. I get the late slip and then I put it in the toilet and I flush it away. I watch it all go away.

I go to the door. But my brain thinks maybe the slip gets back up and someone will see it. Then they will tell on me. I get back to the toilet and then I look. But it doesn't be there. I flush the toilet again. My brain keeps doing it. It doesn't like me to get to the door. I flush the toilet six times and the late slip still doesn't come back. I tell my brain to stop it because it is going to make me cry and I have to go back to my classroom.

I go to my classroom. My teacher asks me why I took lots of time. I say I have tummy ache and I went to the toilet. It is all gone now. She tells me to sit down and then start my school work.

I take the register lots of days if I don't be very late. Then I give it to the office lady and I change it all the time. I don't ever get shouted at about it. Sometimes, I get to school too late and then the register already gets to the office. I put the slip in the toilet. No one ever gets to know about it. I do those lots of times too.

It gets to be a Friday and I sit on the chair and my dad sits on the sofa and he does the stare thing. I don't like when my dad does the stare thing. I feel all bad inside because maybe I am in trouble and I don't know about it. I hug my school bag very tight. I don't even get my uniform off. My mum doesn't ever let me sit down with my uniform on. It gets to go in the wash pile right away.

My dad gets his angry eyes. He has a piece of paper in his hand. He screws it up into a ball and he throws it at me and it hits me in the face. I squeeze myself together and my tummy gets the sick feeling inside. I don't know what I have done. Maybe it is my badness.

"Why haven't you been going to school?" he asks.

I tell him I do. My dad gets up and then he gets the paper and he makes it flat again. He does it fast because he is mad at me. He smacks it on my legs. It gets lots of dates on it. They all say that I don't be in school that day. But I do. I always get to school. I just was late.

"It says that you weren't at school in the mornings."

He stands up all big and tall.

"Where did you go?"

I tell him I was at school and he says I am a liar.

I tell him I wasn't. I tell him that I just be late because we don't leave the house very early. My dad bends down and bangs his hands on the arms of the chair. He gets to talk in my face.

"Is that my fault?"

I shake my head very hard. It doesn't be. It is mine. I am bad.

My dad gets my school bag. He goes inside it and he gets my book. He pulls the pages out of it.

STUPID BOY

Then he put them in the fireplace and lights them
on fire with his lighter. I tell him no. I tell him to
stop it. I try to stand up but my dad does the stare
thing. I sit back down.

THIRTEEN

One day, Stupid Boy's mum and dad was very happy. They got to be all excited in their tummies and it made them have huge giant big smiles on their faces. The nice lady was going to come home because the doctors had made her all better and then they got to take Stupid Boy back and they didn't have to be bothered about his stupids anymore.

The End.

I am sad. I don't get to play with my friends Andrew and Sheba anymore. But I like my Nan coming home. I am sad I have to say goodbye to Sheba and Andrew. They don't get to live at my Nan's house. Only me and Mr. Ted live there. Then the bad man doesn't get them too.

My Nan's house is scary. It is like a big monster house. Maybe all the children don't go there because they get ate up. I stand outside the gate and stare at the window. Maybe the curtain moved. Maybe the bad man is watching and can see me and he is waiting. Maybe when my Nan opens the door the bad man will eat her all up.

My Nan gives me a sweet. It is all hard and I keep it in my mouth until it is all small. I am stupid and I try to bite it. It makes a crack noise in my mouth. Like snap crackle and pop.

STUPID BOY

I am stupid. I think I have got my tooth all broken. It makes me sad in my tummy and I start to cry.

My Nan looks inside my mouth.

"You've just made it wobbly," she says. "It will fall out and then the tooth fairy will buy it from you."

Tooth fairy? I never get to give my teeth to her. She thinks my teeth are stinky and bad and the dentist man puts them in the rubbish bin.

I ask my Nan if it is true that the fairy buys teeth, and she nods and smiles and says that it is.

"Just wait and see," she says.

I wiggle my tooth. I think about the tooth fairy. Maybe the tooth will get to fall out and then I can sell it to her.

I wish my tooth gets to fall out. But it doesn't. It just stays in my mouth and then it wobbles and I make my tongue make it wiggle about but it doesn't want to fall out.

It is the next day and my mum comes to the house to see if my Nan is better. I show my mum my tooth and she calls the dentist. We get to go there when I finish school so he can look at it. My mum says that I go to the dentist because maybe the bit inside needs to get taken out.

I don't like to see the dentist. He makes me scared in my tummy and he gives me stupid stinky gas that makes me fall to sleep. Then I get sick in my tummy from it and my mum gets mad about it. But the dentist after school says he is just going to have a look at it. He tells me to open my mouth all big and wide. He wants to look at all my teeth.

He says the front one is wobbly and it will fall out by itself. He says I shouldn't eat lots of hard sweets because I will make all my teeth break. Maybe then I can be like a monster and have lots of sharp teeth and I can bite people. Like the bad man does. He has lots of sharp teeth and when he bites me it hurts very bad and makes me cry. I don't want to make people cry though.

I go back to the dentist at the end of the week. Then he can look and see if my wobbly tooth has falled out. He says he wants to look at a tooth all the way at the back. But it doesn't be wobbly. He says it gets a hole on it.

I keep playing with my tooth. Maybe I can make it fall out if I wiggle it lots of times.

Me and my Nan are going on a train when it gets to the next morning. She says maybe the train will go very fast and make my tooth all shake out. I hope so.

We are going to go and see a lady. She is called Auntie Annie. She is my Nan's auntie. I have some of those but I don't get to see them. Auntie Annie lives somewhere that is a long way away and we have to get on a train because my Nan doesn't be able to drive a car. We don't tell my mum and dad we are going out. My mum doesn't like Auntie Annie. She says she is all mean inside. Maybe she gets some badness too like me and my Nan.

STUPID BOY

I don't get allowed to take Mr. Ted with me. My Nan says it is a long way and then if he gets left behind maybe I don't be able to get him back. I tell Andrew he can come though. But I don't tell my Nan about Andrew. He is invisible so she doesn't be able to see him and she won't get to say no about it. Me and Andrew don't ever get to be on a train before.

We have to get up very early. We have to get a taxi too. It has to take us to the train station and then we get to sit. My Nan lets me take some paper and pencils and me and Andrew get to draw and make stories. I will tell Mr. Ted about them when we get home again.

We are going to write about the train. It is very fast. I draw a picture of it. Andrew says that maybe I should draw a monster on top of the train. He breaks in with his claws and he is big and makes lots of growl noises. He will eat all the people on the train and we run away and live in the forest.

We get to the place where Auntie Annie lives. It is a place called Bolton. My Nan says it is where she gets to live when she was a little girl. I didn't know my Nan ever gets to be a little girl. Her mum and dad are in heaven like Gaga. She says Auntie Annie is her mum's sister. My mum's got a sister too.

We stay at Auntie Annie's house all day long. She is a nice lady and I don't see her badness. Maybe she keeps it away or maybe she has some medicine and then it gets all better and she doesn't have it any more.

She looks at my tooth. She says maybe I can put a string on it and pull it out. She says the tooth fairy will pay lots of money for my tooth.

Me and Andrew play outside. She has a nice back garden and we play living in the forest from the monster on the train. My Nan makes me some sandwiches and she says I can eat them outside. Andrew doesn't like sandwiches. Not the ones I get. He gets his own. He makes them himself because he doesn't have a mum and dad. They ran away like mine did. Andrew is all big and clever and gets to make all his things by himself.

I bite my sandwich. It gets all red and then Andrew says it is my tooth. I feel it. It has fallen out and it is in my mouth with my sandwich. I spit it all out in my hand. My tooth has got out. I am happy about it.

I take it inside and show my Nan and she has a big smile too. She puts it in a tissue and in her bag. She says we will put it under the pillow when it is night time because that is when the tooth fairy comes so no one get to see her.

We ride on the train again to go home. Andrew doesn't be with us. He is tired and he went home all by himself. I sit with my Nan. I am tired too and I lean on her and my eyes want to go to sleep all the way home. I am tired in the taxi too. But I don't sleep in that.

STUPID BOY

My mum is at my Nan's house. She has her angry eyes. She is waiting for us in the front garden. I don't know what I have done. Maybe my badness got out and I don't know about it. My mum is smoking her cigarette and my dad is sitting in the car.

I show my mum my mouth and tell her about my tooth.

"Shut up and get in the house," she says.

My tummy does its turn over thing. I don't want to go in the house all by myself. Maybe the bad man is hiding in there. But my Nan comes in too and it is okay. There doesn't be any bad man downstairs in the back room.

My Nan sits in her chair by the fire and my mum is very mad. She shouts bad words and calls my Nan bad names. She says she is big and fat and stinky. I don't think my Nan is big or fat or stinky. She is nice. I sit next to my Nan's feet. My mum doesn't be mad at me, but she makes my tummy all scared inside.

My mum tries to get my Nan's hand and make her stand up. Maybe she is going to send my Nan away to the bedroom like she does when I am bad. But my Nan is big and my mum doesn't be able to make her stand up. It makes my mum even lots more mad about it. And she shouts so loud that I don't know what she is saying.

My Nan tells her to get off her hand and my mum hits my Nan. My Nan pushes my mum away and my mum falls into the fire. It doesn't be on, but she gets all hurt and cries about it. My Nan stands up and maybe my Nan is going to hit my mum like my dad does when he is mad and then he does it lots of times.

I try to hug my mum and I tell my Nan to stop it. She doesn't be allowed to hit my mum. I don't be able to keep all the crying away. I don't want them to get hurt. My mum pushes me and I fall over too. She stands up and she says bad words to me and my Nan and then she goes away and makes the house all shake and nearly fall down when she makes the door all slam closed.

FOURTEEN

One day, Stupid Boy gets to go to the dentist. He don't like to go there. It makes him scared in his tummy. He don't like when the dentist puts the mask on his face and then he gets to smell the stinky gas that makes everyone fall to sleep.

When Stupid Boy gets to wake up again. All his teeth have got pulled out and then he don't be able to eat any food. He gets to starve until he dies.

The End.

My mum says I have to go to the dentist again. He has to look at my back tooth and he wants to look at the hole where the one that falled out is. My mum says the one at the back has to be pulled out. I put my tongue on it and make it move. But it doesn't be wobbly. I tell my mum it doesn't want to come out. But she says that it has to.

I look at it in the mirror. I open my mouth all wide. I don't know why the dentist wants to take my tooth out. My dad comes and looks too and he says that the dentist is going to get some things called pliers like he uses on his bike and he will pull the tooth right out of my mouth.

I don't want the dentist to put bike pliers in my mouth. I ask Mr. Ted if it is true. But he doesn't know. He doesn't ever go to the dentist. He doesn't get to open his mouth. Andrew doesn't go to the dentist either because he is invisible. I ask Sheba about it. She has lots and lots of teeth in her mouth. I put my fingers at the side and then she opens her mouth big and wide and I get to see her teeth. She has stinky breath and gets the slobber all on my hands. Maybe she doesn't go to the dentist either.

I have a story book about the dentist. It is about Tim and Tom. Tim has a poorly tooth and then the dentist took it out and makes it all better. The tooth fairy comes and then he gets a new tooth. My tooth doesn't be poorly though. I don't want to get it out.

The dentist place smells all funny. It is like a house. Maybe the dentist lives there. I don't want to live at a dentist house. I don't like the smell of all the gas. Me and my mum walk to the dentist. It isn't very far from my Nan's house. I walk past my school and all the children are playing in the yard. I don't go to school because I have the dentist. I wish I could play with my friends instead.

My mum says I am going to have the gas. I don't like it. It makes me fall to sleep. Then when I wake up it makes me feel all sick in my tummy and my mum will be mad about that. She doesn't like when the sick comes out because she has to clean it up and she is very busy all the time.

My mum says my Nan doesn't clean the sick up. She says if I get sick when she has gone back home then my Nan will just leave the sick on the floor. Then it will be a "stinking pile of crap on the floor." I don't want to make any piles of crap on the floor.

My mum is scared when we walk. She doesn't like the walking part because she says something bad is going to happen. She gets to feel it in her intuition. I don't know where the intuition is. Maybe it is in her tummy. I have bats in my tummy. That's what my Nan says. They fly around and make growl sounds. I didn't ever hear my mum's intuition make any growl sounds. Maybe it is like Andrew and Mr. Ted. It talks to her in secret about things and no one else gets to hear. My mum says it tells her not to go out and then when she does she gets scared about it.

My mum says we have to walk on the left side of the road. Then nothing bad gets to happen to us. If we walk on the right then maybe my mum will get sick too. Then maybe she will get to die and go to heaven. I don't want her to go to heaven.

We get inside the dentist house and we get to sit in the waiting room. My mum reads the magazines and I am not allowed to talk to her because she has to pretend that she isn't out somewhere. Then she doesn't get scared about it. I sit on the chair and be all quiet until the lady comes and says it is my turn.

My mum doesn't come with me. When the lady says my name then my mum smiles at the lady and tells me to go on. I have tummy ache.

The dentist chair is all big and black. There are two dentists and a nurse. The dentist says he wants to look in my mouth first and he does. He gets the mirror thing and then he looks and he shows the other dentist. I tell him it isn't wobbly. He says it has a hole in it and will make my mouth sore.

The nurse asks if I want to take my tooth home after. She says I can get a little envelope. They will sign it to say I am brave and maybe the tooth fairy will come. I tell her yes please. Me and Mr. Ted like the tooth fairy. Maybe Mr. Ted doesn't scare her away like he does with the bad man sometimes.

I wish the tooth fairy will come. When I had my wobbly tooth out she got in the bedroom. She didn't wake me up and then she put fifty pence under my pillow and I got to spend it on a new car. I put it with all the cars I got from Graham.

The dentist says they are going to put the mask on my face and then I will be done and be able to go home again. I don't like the mask. I don't be able to breathe. My brain wants to see the pictures of the bad man and his big dark hands. It makes my heart go all fast, but I don't cry.

"How old are you?" The nurse asks.

I tell her I am seven.

"Is your birthday soon?"

I shake my head. It is ages and ages to wait.

"Did you get lots of presents on your last birthday?"

I try to shake my head.

STUPID BOY

The mask smells funny inside. It makes my head feel all dizzy and there is lots of colours. Maybe I am going to fall off the chair. I hold my breath and then I don't get to breath it all in.

The dentist says that I am supposed to go to sleep and then the other dentist asks to look at the mask. Maybe it doesn't work properly. He puts it on again and then he gets his hand on my mouth. I don't get able to breathe through there instead. They say they is just going to give me some more and everything is okay.

I don't know that I have walked out of the dentist. I don't know that my tooth has got out. My mum yells my name and tells me that I better wake up or there is going to be trouble. But my legs are tired and my eyes want to go to sleep.

"I'm not going to carry you home. Get up," she says.

I get to feel poorly in my tummy. It does the flip over thing and then I need to get the sick out. My mum grabs my arm and she pushes me at the kerb.

"You better be sick in the gutter," she says. "Or else."

It comes out and my mouth bleeds too. I wish I am like magic and then I can just make myself get home again.

My mum says lots of swear words at me. She doesn't like having to take me to the dentist because she always has to do these things and no one cares.

"I have to look after you all time and no one helps me. I wish you would go away," she says.

I wish I will go away too.

Stupid Boy.

I am too sleepy to walk. I sit down. My mum shouts at me.

"Get up."

My legs are like jelly. Maybe they will go invisible again.

"If you don't get up right now, I am going to leave you here."

I shake my head. I tell my mum I am too tired.

"Stay there then. I don't care."

She says the swear words at me and then she walks away and leaves me to sit there.

Maybe there is a place for little boys when their mums don't want them. Maybe they get throwed away. Maybe those little boys don't have Mr. Teds like me. I am lucky to have him. I wish he is with me. I miss him. But he is at home in bed because I don't be allowed to take him to the dentist.

I say mum lots of times. I say it three times and then three times more. But she doesn't come back. I squeeze my knees up but I don't let my eyes cry. I am bad and then she doesn't want me. She walks up the road and she doesn't come back. Maybe I will get lost forever. I say her name three more times, but then the sick wants to come out at the same time. It makes my head want to go pop. But my mum doesn't come back.

Maybe my mum doesn't ever come back.

My legs don't want to walk but I make them do it. I wish I had Sheba with me. Maybe she will help me get home to my Nan's house again. There are lots of walls and things that I lean on and I don't get shouted at about it. I say mum lots more times. Maybe she will get to hear me and come back. Then I can tell her that I am sorry and I don't mean to get sick or make her stay outside for a long time.

I say it over and over.

I get to the shop that is near my school. The one I get to meet my mum at sometimes. She is there and she is waiting for me. She stands there with her cigarette and talks to her friend. She tells me to hurry so we can walk home. She has lots to do.

We get home and I lie by the fire and go to sleep. My mum is gone when I wake up.

She didn't say goodbye.

FIFTEEN

Everyone in the land knew that behind the big long curtains, lived the curtain monster. He was the ugliest monster in the world. He had big bony hands that feeled like cold sticks. He got big hair that was like lots of dead worms. His teeth were the biggest and sharpest ever.

No one liked him.

He came at the dark time to the houses where the bad boys lived. He hided there and got them when they did bad things and then he bit them and scratched them and made them be sorry.

The End.

I have a curtain monster. He comes because I am an evil boy. I know that he is there and me and Sheba and Andrew and Mr. Ted get our swords and are ready to chop the curtain monsters head off. We watch and we wait. Maybe he doesn't come tonight.

Stupid Boy is ready.

The monster comes with his sharp nails and his pointy chin. He has big yellow eyes. I don't hear the monster sneak up on me. He grabs me and tries to hurt me. He bites me and maybe he will make me into a monster too. I scream and shout as loud as I can.

Andrew, Mr. Ted and Sheba all come. We chop the monster into a million pieces and then we throw him out the window and the evil black cat eats him all up.

I like that I get to live with my Nan again. Me and Mr. Ted is happy that she don't get to go to heaven to see Gaga. I like that I don't have to see the stupid office lady with her shouting at me because I am late. I don't be late again when I live at my Nan's house.

I get to get sleepovers at my mum and dad's house again on the weekends. I don't be bad because they don't get to see me all the time and then they don't get sick and tired of all my badness.

It gets to Sunday and I get to feel sad in my tummy because when it is after dinner time, they take me back to my Nan's house and leave me there.

My mum and dad let me stay in bed. I am very tired. Maybe it is all the fighting with the bad man in the curtains. He didn't come. But I know he is there and I watch all night long so he doesn't be able to jump out and get me.

I don't know if I am allowed to stay in bed or if I am allowed to get up and go and play. Maybe I will get shouted at if I stay in bed all day long and be lazy. Even Sheba has got out of bed and she doesn't be at the door. It is just me and Mr. Ted. I don't know where Andrew is. Maybe he keeps away because I feel sad inside. He doesn't ever come and play when I am sad inside.

My mum and dad are in the lounge. They have coffee and they are eating bacon sandwiches. My dad says I can have one and it is in the kitchen but maybe it has got cold now. I go into the kitchen and I get coffee too. I don't like it very much. But I put lots and lots of sugar in it and then it is nice. My Nan says when I have lots of sugar I will get worms. I don't know what she means. Ants like sugar, not worms. I don't ever see worms in sugar. Maybe she is being silly like my dad does sometimes.

I get my bacon sandwich and I eat it all up and then I go back in the lounge. I am not allowed to eat in there. I have to eat at the big kitchen table and then I don't make a mess. Mr. Ted sits with me. But he doesn't get any bacon because he doesn't like it.

My mum tells me to come and sit with them on the sofa. They don't be mad at me about staying in bed. They don't tell me that I am lazy. Maybe they are happy. Maybe my badness didn't come out. My dad puts his arms out. His sleeve is all big and over his hand. I don't know why he does it. My mum tells me to pull it off.

I pull it and then my dad does the same at the other side so I pull that too. Then I take his jumper off. My dad has a shirt on too. He does the sleeve thing with it. My mum says I have to get all the buttons open. She helps me too because they are all little and I am not very good with them.

STUPID BOY

"Take off the belt, shoes and pants too," she says.

My mum gets a bag and she gives it to me. It has something white inside it. I don't know what it is. It looks funny. It looks like a bra that is all big. Me and my mum take my dad's underwear off and then we put the bra thing on him. It is so big that it gets everywhere. It is like a swimming suit that my mum wears. There's a big hole at the bottom and it is for his thing to come out.

I don't know what I am supposed to do. They don't talk to me and tell me. My dad sits there in the funny clothes and stares at me. But not the stare thing. He doesn't be mad at me.

But then my badness comes out and I don't know it is there. I don't know I am going to be bad. Maybe it sneaks up on me like a curtain monster.

My dad holds his hands out to me and then my badness comes from the devil part. I don't mean to make my dad hurt. It is on accident when my badness makes me kick him with my foot. I kick my dad so hard in his thing and he shouts very loud.

He gets his fist and punches me in the tummy and I fall back and fall over. I don't be able to breathe. I try to but it hurts too bad. I don't be able to cry either because I don't be able to breathe.

My mum gets mad. She shouts at me. "What are you doing?"

She shouts at my dad too and asks him why it has got this way. I try to tell my dad I am sorry. I don't mean to kick him. But he is mad and he sits there and maybe I hurt him very bad.

My mum picks me up and tells me it is bad to kick people there because I can make them die. She rubs my back so I can breathe. I cry and I tell her I am sorry. I didn't mean to do it.

My mum goes to my dad and she gives him a big hug too. He doesn't cry. He isn't a big baby like me. I am stupid and a baby and I cry all the time and then I hurt my dad. Maybe the bad man should chop me into lots of pieces and feed me to the black cat.

My dad takes my mum's clothes off. But he doesn't put any funny clothes on her. She sits on his knee and then they do the grown up thing on the sofa. It is like the hurt thing, but my dad doesn't hurt my mum with it. It is what grownups do like in the television things me and my dad watch.

STUPID BOY

SIXTEEN

Stupid Boy told Mr. Ted that he missed Sheba very much. He wished he got to play with her. Maybe she would want to be a dragon again.

Mr. Ted said to Stupid Boy, "Why don't you go to the old man's house and see Snoopy?"

Stupid Boy thought that Mr. Ted had a very good idea. The old man's house was quiet outside. Stupid Boy knocked on the door.

One.

Two.

Three.

No one got to answer the door.

Stupid Boy looked through the window. Maybe the old man had gone out.

The old lady that lived in the blue house next door came out. She had a very sad face. The old man had gone to heaven too.

Stupid Boy felt sad in his tummy.

The End.

I wish it is lunch time. My mum and dad say that Peter can come and play and then he is going to go home again when I go to my Nan's. His mum is going to bring him and then she is going to have coffee and talk about all the boring things while me and Peter play. He is bringing his bike too. I don't be able to wait. It makes me wake up before everyone in the house. It is miles of hours away.

My dad wakes up and then he gets out of bed. I don't get up. Maybe I don't be allowed to yet. But I wish he would say I can. Then I will go and play outside and wait for Peter to come. Maybe I will be able to go to the bridge and wait for his mum's car. Then we can ride down the lanes. But I won't go on the sand. Maybe there are trolls. Me and Peter say maybe one day we can go there and catch one and then tie it up and keep it forever.

My dad doesn't say I am allowed to get out of bed. He goes downstairs and then he comes back up again. He has made coffee for my mum and brought it upstairs. They lie there and talk about lots of things and drink their coffee.

My dad asks me if I am awake. Maybe I am in some trouble. I hug Mr. Ted and then we sit up and say yes. My dad says he has made me some coffee too and I can have it if I am good. Me and Mr. Ted are very happy about that. We get out of bed and then we make it all straight so my mum doesn't have to do it.

I climb over my dad and get in the bed. It is all warm in the middle and it is very special to be there. Mr. Ted thinks so too. My dad gives me the coffee. He makes it with milk and lots of sugar. It is very nice but I don't like the skin bit on the top. My mum tells me to stop sticking my fingers in the coffee. But I don't want it to touch my mouth when I am drinking. I move it when she doesn't look.

My dad tells me that my feet are all cold and then he makes a noise when they touch his leg. I move my feet away and then he doesn't get mad about it. But my mum gets her feet and puts them on my dad and laughs about it. My dad grabs my mum's foot and tickles it. She screams and then it knocks my coffee and I spill some on my top.

I sit very still. My mum gets mad when I spill things but my dad says it is okay. I tell my mum I am sorry about it.

"Just take it off and go put it on your bed. It'll dry," she says.

I get my top off and my dad puts it on my bed for me. I finish my coffee and then my dad puts my cup on the floor. My dad is silly. He gets in the bed again. There don't be any coffee and he tickles my mum and then tickles me too. I try to get away but he is all big and his arms grab me. I don't be able to get out of the bed.

My dad sits on me so I don't be able to move. He tickles my tummy and makes me scream at him about it. I tell him to tickle my mum instead but he keeps getting me and I don't be able to stop the laughing. It makes my tummy all hurt inside and my eyes get to cry. But they aren't sad.

Then my dad jumps on my mum too. He holds her down and he tickles her. He tells me to help and she screams and laughs and says bad words. But she doesn't be mad. My dad laughs and tickles her more.

My dad gets some shoe laces and then he gets my hands and he put them down by my sides so I don't be able to lift them up. My dad is very strong. He ties up my hands with the laces and then ties them to the top of the bed. Then he tickles me so bad that maybe if he don't stop I will have to go to the toilet. I scream for him to stop it. I don't be able to laugh any more. It doesn't want to come out and it makes my tummy all hurt and then I can't breathe.

My dad stops but he is laughing and then he gets my mum's hands and ties them up too. My dad says that he can tickle us forever and there is nothing we can do about it.

He gets on the funny underwear thing again because my mum tells him to. But he has to do it himself because we are all tied up.

My dad pretends to be like the curtain monster and he is going to get us. I try to get my hands out but they are all tied up. My dad gets a monster voice too and he gets on the bed. Sometimes my dad is silly. He hits my mum in the face with his thing and she laughs about it. He makes me laugh too and I try to keep my face away from him when he gets to me. He tries to hit me too. I laugh and tell him to stop it. He keeps trying to get his thing in our mouths. I tell him to get my mum and she tells him to get me. She is better at the game than me though. My dad tries to trick us and then he is too fast for me. He gets it in my mouth and I don't be able to get it away. My mum and dad laugh about it and I try to get my head away but I can't.

STUPID BOY

After my dad does the yucky part in my mouth, we all laugh. It makes me cough and my dad tells me not to get the sick out. I don't. I am very good at not getting the sick out. I swallow lots of times and then my mum doesn't get mad about it.

My dad says I am a good boy. I smile at that. I ask my dad if I can go and get ready because soon Peter will be there. I don't want to not have my bike and things out. My dad says yes. But I have to go to the bathroom first.

I don't know why my eyes want to cry. I have been playing with my mum and dad. But when I get into the hallway my eyes keep letting the tears out. Stupid Boy gets to cry and be a baby because he lost the game.

I get in the bathroom and I look at the stupid boy. I say bad words to him and tell him to stop it.

SEVENTEEN

Stupid Boy and his friend got their bikes. They rided them a long, long way until they came to the big gates. Big giant gates. Stupid Boy and his friend looked through them.

That was where the Troll king lived. He keeped all the children in there and he keeped them as slaves. They looked very hard to see the slaves. Maybe they could save them and keep them all safe.

Stupid Boy's friend pointed.

"Look there," he said.

Stupid Boy and his friend looked. There was a cat. It was big and it was black and it had monster eyes. The evil black cat.

He saw Stupid Boy and his friend then he made them fall to sleep with his gas breath. He could chop them into bits.

The End.

Peter is staying at my mum and dad's house with me because I have been a good boy. I don't tell him about the game that I played with my mum and dad. I don't talk about it even to Andrew or Sheba. Just Mr. Ted. But not a lot. It makes me feel bad because I do all the bad things.

My badness makes me do bad things. I go in the bathroom before Peter comes. I get my dad's razor and I make a line with it in my hair. Andrew says to do it there and then no one can see. I do it above my ear. I make the Stupid Boy hurt. I don't let Peter see it.

Peter has got his bike with him. I have my bike that my dad has got for me. We get to ride very fast on the lanes. My dad says that when we are on the lanes we have to ride on the wrong side of the road. If we ride on the wrong side then no one can hit us with their cars.

There is a big house down the lane. It is big and giant. It is next to a field. There is a big ugly bull in the field. My dad says I don't be allowed in there. He says that the bull will get me with his horns and then all my blood will get out. I don't want all my blood to get out. But I like looking at the bull. He stands there when I talk to him. He doesn't say anything. Maybe he doesn't know how to be magic.

Peter says maybe the big house is where they get people and keep them forever. Maybe they make them slaves and they get to do all the boring things. If they don't do them, then they get their heads chopped off. That is why they have the big gates. Then the people don't get to run away. Not ever.

We are going to climb over the gate. We want to go and get to the house. Then we can look in the windows and see the people they have there. We get our bikes and then we put them under the bushes. There is a hole there too. We don't have to get over the gates. We get through the hole instead.

Maybe someone tried escape already. Maybe they got out of the hole and then the trolls got them.

Me and Peter crawl on the ground. We hide under the bushes. We are going to get to the windows and look. Maybe there will be dead people. Peter doesn't want to see dead people. He doesn't like them.

There is a big car there too. When we get to the house Peter says maybe the car is the boss's car. And then he sits there and sees us through the cameras. We don't want him to see us. Maybe he will come out and get us and make us into monsters.

Peter is scared in his tummy about it. Maybe we won't be allowed to go home again. He doesn't want to look at the house. I tell him it is okay. We run back to our bikes. We never ever go there again.

Me and Peter play on our bikes all day long. At dinner time my mum makes a big salad. My dad gets some fish things. He says they are called kippers. He cooks them under the grill. They smell all smoky. My dad gets the kipper and then he pulls all the bones out in one go. He shows me how to do it.

I get the end of the kipper. Then I pull it. But I do it slow and in a special way. I get all the bones out together. I show Peter my kipper skeleton. He thinks it looks funny. My dad says I have to throw it away. He says that if Sheba or the cats get it maybe they will choke. I don't want them to choke.

I show my mum the kipper skeleton. She doesn't like it.

"Damn kippers do nothing but stink the place out," she says.

She has her mad face and tells my dad he shouldn't let me play with the food. "He'll make it dirty," she says. "Then I have to clean up all this mess.

She doesn't like the kippers because they make a smell everywhere. She tells my dad he doesn't be allowed them.

Me and Peter have to take our kippers outside. We eat salad too. We take our plates to the pond. There is an island in the middle. It is all full of grass. Me and Sheba have made it all flat. There is a plank to stand on too. I got it from the climbing thing at the front. We walk on it and then me and Peter sit on the island and eat our dinner. Maybe we are like pirates.

The kippers are very nice. Peter likes them too. I tell my dad they are nice. I say thank you very much and I put my plate in the wash. My dad says if I am good I can have some on the next weekend. Some just for me. I tell him I will.

It gets to be dark time and my dad is going to take Sheba for a walk before he goes to bed. Me and Peter ask if we can go. I like to do the walk at night when it is dark. There are bats in the sky. My dad lets us put skates on. We get big giant torches too. Me and Peter race up and down the lane. We don't go very far. My dad says we aren't allowed.

After we take Sheba for a walk it is bedtime. We are allowed to stay awake. But we have to be very quiet. We are camping in the bedroom that is next to my mum and dad's room. It is my room. Where they put my things. But I don't get to stay there. Only when Peter comes for a sleepover.

My mum says I have to go to the toilet to brush my teeth and wash my face before I go to bed. I have to do it every night. But my dad is in the shower. I don't like to go in the bathroom when Peter is there. I don't like to go in the bathroom when my dad is in the shower. But it is the time I am allowed there. Then my dad knows I wasn't being bad.

Peter waits in my bedroom. He waits with Sheba and Mr. Ted. He is going to make the tent nice and get his pyjamas on. I have to get my pyjamas on in the bathroom. Then I put my dirty clothes with the washing pile and not on the bedroom floor. Peter puts his dirty clothes in a bag.

I use the toilet and take my clothes off. I put my pyjamas on. My dad does his stare thing. Not the angry stare thing. It is a different stare thing. It makes me feel my badness inside my tummy and all over my skin. I wish my dad don't be there then I can make Stupid Boy hurt with the razor.

Maybe my badness will come out and my dad will do the hurt thing. But then my dad smiles at me and makes a sucky noise and sticks his finger in his mouth. I wish my dad didn't know about my badness. It makes him do the hurt thing. I wish he didn't know about that. I wish I get to be able to cut it all away.

I make my teeth clean and I wash my face. I wash my hands and I make my nails scratch. It gets to hurt and scratch away my badness. Like the bad man does. He makes it go away.

I get the towel all in a nice line so my mum doesn't be mad or the bad man doesn't come.

My dad goes to bed too. It isn't his bedtime. But he is going to read a story to my brother. I tells him goodnight and then I go to my room and play camping with Peter.

EIGHTEEN

The evil black cat did not be able to get into the garden. He tried. He tried lots of times. Andrew and Stupid Boy got to sit on the cat and scare him away. The evil black cat wanted to get in and then he was going to steal Susie back and keep her as a slave. He would put her in the dungeon.

Susie cat liked Stupid Boy. She asked Stupid Boy to help save her brother and sister. No one else in the land was brave enough to do it. Stupid Boy was going to make a trap and then they would catch the evil black cat and make him give back Tuppence and Penny.

The End.

We sit on the big tall part of the gate. We have our big swords with us and we wait for the evil black cat to come. We hear him coming.

We get down on the ground and then we can hear his claws on the wood when he gets so high. We are ready. We can make his head chopped off and all the other cats will be let go.

It isn't the evil black cat that got over the gate. It is the cat with no name. He is so mean no one ever called him anything.

I tell Andrew and Mr. Ted we should hide. We will need lots of magic to catch the cat with no name. He is big and strong and he has claws that are bigger than the sword.

STUPID BOY

Mr. Ted thinks that I am right.

I hug Susie and we all hide. We tell her we will keep her safe forever.

The cat with no name goes away.

Andrew says he has a plan and he will tell us about it later.

My mum and dad's house has big gates at the front of it. There is a big fence too. There are lots of trees and then no one can see inside. There is a big driveway that is made of things called cobbles.

When the gates are all closed then my mum and dad get to sunbathe. They lie on a blanket. It is a nice warm day and my dad lies there and reads his book. My mum gets her music on and closes her eyes and then tries to make herself all brown. I play in the trees and be quiet and my brother plays in his paddling pool that is next to them.

My mum and dad always lie in the sun with no clothes on. Not even any underwear. They like to sunbathe like that. They do it lots of times. They don't be shy.

My mum doesn't get mad at me when I get my book and sit next to them on the grass and read it. She goes in the house and gets some drinks. She makes them all cold and when she comes outside again she gives one to me and one to my brother. They are very nice and I say thank you for it. Then she smiles because I remember not to be bad. She gets my dad his special drink too. He makes it himself. It is wine and it is red. My mum calls it plonk.

My mum sits down again. But she doesn't lie down. Maybe she doesn't be tired any more. She gets my hand and tells me to put it on my dad. I don't know what she means and then she shows me. I put my hand on his tummy. It is all hot and sticky. I don't like it because his tummy is hairy. It feels funny being there and maybe she will let me take my hand off.

But my mum puts my hand on my dad's thing. I don't like it being there either. I don't want to look at it. I look at the grass.

My mum has some bottles of nail varnish there. She has made her toe nails all nice. I pick one up and play with it. My mum doesn't shout at me about it. She keeps moving my hand on my dad's thing. I don't want to see. I don't want to look at my brother or my dad or my mum because I am all bad.

I get my mum's bottle of nail varnish and I get the top open. I pour it on my dad's thing because maybe it will be funny to draw on him. I don't know that it will get to hurt him. My dad jumps up very high and then he starts to scream and hold his thing. Maybe everyone can hear him.

My badness always makes me do the bad things. I don't mean to do them. It is something in my brain. Maybe there is a monster in there. But it always gets the bad thoughts and then sometimes I do them and I don't know why. I am just bad. My dad is right that I am too bad. Maybe they will be better to give me away forever.

My brother starts crying because my mum shouts at me and my dad runs into the house. He is shouting and screaming and he is all mad. I am in big trouble. Maybe he will come and hit me because my badness got out again. I don't mean to make my dad hurt. My mum runs in the house too. I don't mean it. It is on accident and I get to cry too.

I squeeze myself together and close my eyes. I wish I could go away. My tummy gets to ache and maybe the sick will come out and my mum will get mad about that too. I shake. I am scared about it because I am bad again. Maybe they will take me back to my Nan's house and then I don't be allowed here again.

My mum comes back out and I ask her if my dad is okay. I tell her I don't know why I did it.

"Maybe you want to leave your father alone when he comes back out," she says. "The nail varnish burnt and it really hurt. You shouldn't have done that."

I didn't mean to burn my dad.

My dad comes back outside. He has his jeans on and he stands there. I don't want to look at him. Maybe he does the stare thing at me.

He doesn't shout at me. He doesn't say anything. I hug myself all up.

Stupid boy.

My dad doesn't talk to me all day. I am just all bad inside. It gets to be bedtime and my dad puts my brother to bed. I ask my dad if I can go too. My dad doesn't say yes. He just holds the door open for me. Then we all go upstairs and my dad reads the book.

My brother falls to sleep and my dad takes my clothes down and does the hurt thing. But he doesn't say anything about it. He doesn't say I am a good boy today. Maybe I am really bad forever.

NINETEEN

Stupid Boy was outside with his mum. They were going to town to get food. They were going to take a trip to the lakes. They needed food to take with them. Then they didn't get to starve to death.

They walked to town because it was nice. Stupid Boy's mum got scared. There were monsters. She was clever and magic and she knew there was one following them. It was behind them. It followed her and then it made bad things happen. It would make her sick in her tummy. She was afraid about the sick from her tummy.

Stupid Boy said he would kill it and no monsters would get her.

Stupid Boy told his mum to hide behind a rock. He got his sword and chopped the monsters head off and then Sheba ate the monster.

The End.

My mum and dad say we are going to go to the lakes if the day is nice. It is two more days and then we will go. I have to stay at my Nan's because it is Thursday and then I have school the next day. But the day after that we are going to the lakes when I get to sleep over.

My mum has to buy the food. Then she gets to make a picnic that we get to sit on the grass and eat. And she has to get milk for my brother. He doesn't have any left for his baby bottles. He doesn't like the picnic very much. But he likes to drink the juice. Sometimes he gets to eat biscuits. My mum buys them for him.

We walk to town. We walk past the doctor's place. Where the nice doctor is. My mum shows me his car. It is big and shiny. He has a new one. My mum says his wife made him buy it. Then when she drives around in it, she gets to say, "Look, I'm the doctor's wife," because she is mean and only wants the money and the big cars. My mum says she is selfish. It is bad to be selfish.

My mum has a skirt on. She asked me if it looked nice. I said it did. My mum always looks nice. She is very pretty. She has a white skirt on and shoes that is high. They make her big. We walk past the doctor's place. She asks me if maybe he can see her walk past. I think maybe he does. Maybe he is shy and doesn't come outside and say hello to her. My mum says he doesn't come and say hello because then his wife will find out and she will take all his money.

We get near town. My mum gets her stare face on. She doesn't be able to talk very much. She squeezes my hand very tight. Maybe she will squeeze all the blood out. She starts to cry. She wants to go home. She gets mad and says bad words. She wishes she didn't go outside. It is a stupid idea. My dad is lazy he should do it. Not her. He gets the car and he should get the food. She shouts lots of things. I tell my mum it is okay. We will go home again.

STUPID BOY

She doesn't be able to breathe. We try to walk very fast. It makes me run. A lady says hello to my mum. My mum doesn't say hello back. Maybe the lady is a nosey old bat. We get home very fast. We get home and my mum tells me to make the door locked and then I give her the keys.

My brother is asleep by the fire. But he wakes up because my Nan asks my mum why we are home.

"Shut up and mind your own damn business," she says to my Nan. "We are home because we want to."

She stands in the kitchen and smokes a cigarette. My Nan tells me to sit at the table and she will make my dinner. I don't have my dinner yet because my mum has picked me up from school.

I like spaghetti and ravioli the best. My Nan asks me what I want and I say I don't know. She makes them both and then she makes egg with it too. I like when I get to open the ravioli and then take the meat part out and then I eat it. I like when the egg is crispy at the edges. But the yellow part is all runny and I put my ravioli in it. My mum comes in the room. She doesn't like when I eat it like that. She says I am playing with my food.

Andrew sits there too. He does the stare thing. Not like my dad. He doesn't do it bad. But he gets to see when I am a stupid boy and then I stop it. Andrew tells me I should eat properly or the bad things happen. I do. But my mum takes my plate away and I don't be finished. She says she has to wash up the dishes before she get to go home.

I ask my mum if I can play outside with my friends. She says yes. I say bye to my mum. But she doesn't say anything to me. She doesn't like to say bye. I say bye to my brother. He says bye. He is awake and drinking his bottle. He has a plate with chocolate biscuits on. I wish I could have them.

I play with my friends Ben and Lawrence. Lawrence lives on the same road as my Nan. He lives all the way at the other end. Next to the little shop. We play out. But he doesn't be allowed off the road. I call for Ben and then we go to see Lawrence and play.

I play out before my mum goes home. Then my Nan doesn't tell me it is time to come in. Then maybe the bad man doesn't get me. I know he is hiding upstairs. He is there and maybe he will make my Nan fall to sleep and he will get me.

I get out before my mum goes and then I get to play until it is nearly time for bed. I have to be back at nine, my mum says. Then it is bedtime at ten and my Nan doesn't send me early.

Me and Ben and Lawrence play outside with the ball. I see my dad. He has Sheba with him. She goes to work with him. He gets my mum and brother and they get in the car. They drive past me. I wave but they don't see me. It makes me feel sad inside. I watch the car go to the corner. I say bye in my head. Maybe they will hear me. Maybe I will be good and they will keep me.

TWENTY

Stupid Boy was very bored. He was bored of his books. He had read them all. He was bored of his toys because he didn't have lots of them. He was bored of everything in the whole world.

He walked downstairs and there was an old man. The old man was bored too. He told Stupid Boy he was sleepy.

Stupid Boy told him, "There is a bed upstairs."

The old man was lost. He didn't know where the upstairs was.

The old man didn't walk very fast. He was like the crooked man that lived in the crooked house with the crooked gate and the crooked dog.

It was a big fat stupid trick.

Stupid Boy was so stupid.

The old man made a sound. He said some words and laughed very loud. It was the curtain monster with the big yellow eyes. He had tricked Stupid Boy. He had come to gobble him all up.

The End.

We are going to the lakes for the day. We have to get up very early because it is a long way to drive and my mum has to make a picnic. Then we have to put it all in the car and we have to drive on the big roads. My dad says it takes a long time to walk up the hill.

I get some special shoes. They are brown and have laces all the way. My dad says they are called walking boots. He says if I get them on and we walk all the long way then my ankles won't hurt or snap off. My dad says they will stop me falling over and breaking my neck.

I don't want to break my neck. Maybe it gets broken and my head will be sideways and I won't be able to lift it up. That will look very stupid. My brother has an action man toy that the neck got broken and his head hangs all down with the wires. Maybe my head will hang down too with the wires in my neck.

I ask my mum about it. She says I am being stupid. I ask Mr. Ted but he doesn't know. We don't want to try it. My brother's action man got put in the rubbish bin because his head didn't get back on. Maybe my head wouldn't go back on and then it will hang sideways forever.

My dad has some walking boots too. His don't have the laces in yet. He used the laces when he tied me and my mum to the bed and played the game. Then he didn't bother to put the laces back in them. He asks me if I will do it. I say I will. I have to do them in a special way so they don't get crossed over. That makes them snap and then my dad's shoes will fall off. Maybe he will break his neck. My dad says he will show me how to do it. Then I can do my mum's too.

STUPID BOY

My mum is in the kitchen. She is making the picnic. She has lots of food. My dad got it because my mum is too scared about it. She shouts at him because he forgot to buy some eggs. Then we don't get to have any boiled eggs in the picnic. And my brother doesn't get any egg for breakfast. My dad says we can go to the farm on the lane and get some. But my mum says bad words to him about it.

My brother sits at the big table. He doesn't talk when my mum and dad is shouting. He has some toast. His toast has honey on it. My dad makes it for him. But he doesn't get lots because he has his baby bottle. My mum wants to get his coat washed. He cries and hugs it when she tries to pick it up. She says he will get honey on it. But it doesn't matter. He wants to keep his coat. My mum says okay.

My dad tells me to go upstairs. His boots are up there. They are under the bed in the bedroom. He comes with me. There isn't any bad man in there. But in my tummy I get scared about it. I look because maybe he is hiding. But I don't see him. Maybe he doesn't be there. The curtains are all open. It is a nice sunny day. He doesn't hide in the curtains. Maybe he doesn't come. He doesn't ever come to my mum and dad's house before. It has been a long time. Maybe Mr. Ted and Sheba and Andrew keeps him away and he is scared.

I feel him there. I know he watches me. He can read my mind and knows if I am bad. Then he will get me when no one is there and no one can hear me scream and cry about it. My brain shows me the pictures about it.

Maybe he will jump out and   hold me down. He will bite me and scratch me. Then he will do the hurt thing and no one will come and help me because I am too bad.

I get scared in my tummy when my dad tells me to get the shoes. They are under the bed. Maybe the bad man is hiding there. My brain has lots of pictures about him. His big eyes and his stinky smile that is all bad. Then he hurts me and my dad doesn't be able to help about it.

The bad man isn't hiding under the bed. It is just lots of shoes. My dad gets to look under the bed too. Maybe he is looking for the bad man. He doesn't see anything and he doesn't get anything. Just his boots and my mum's boots. They are the same as mine. Just bigger. He says I have to put the laces in so they went in a line all across.

I get his boots and then I get the laces and I make them go in. My dad says we are going to the hills that we have passed lots of times. He says it is a long walk. He talks about it and then my tummy gets to all freeze up because my dad gets my pants open. I don't look at them. Then he doesn't know that I know about it and then he won't think I am all bad inside.

My dad gets his boots and puts them on the bed. He says it is easier to do them there. I kneel and make the laces all nice. My dad keeps telling me about the hills. He says there are some caves. Maybe next time we can go to the caves and see if we are able to find some trolls. I don't want to go there. I don't like trolls. I don't ever want to see them.

My dad gets his pants open and leans on me on the bed. He does the hurt thing but I keep putting the laces in the shoes. I don't want my dad to know about the hurt thing. He will think I am very bad inside and then he will send me away because of all the bad things I do. He won't like me because of the hurt thing. I feel all yucky inside about it. I get the laces in the boots slowly. Then I don't have to look anywhere. And I don't think about the hurt thing.

My dad makes his funny noise. I don't like when he does that because it hurts more. Then my dad stands up and puts his pants back up. He takes his boots too. I have got the laces all nice. I just have my mum's to do. My dad goes downstairs.

I get my nails and then I hug my arms very tight. I make them scratch all the way down. It keeps my eyes from doing the crying. I don't get to cry. I am so bad inside. I wish I could scratch it all away. I stand up and it hurts inside too. I tell myself good. It is good it hurts inside. It should hurt inside. Stupid boy that does the hurt thing. I hate him. I wish he hurt very bad forever. It is good. I pull my hair. I wish I can pull it all out and then pull my head off.

I make it all scratchy in my nose when I get to breathe. I count. I count to six. Six scratches and I pull my hair when I do it. I pull so hard my stupid eyes get to cry about it. I keep doing it. Then my mum shouts me and asks for her boots.

STUPID BOY

TWENTY ONE

Stupid Boy and his friends all went out for the day. They went to the big hills that touched the sky. They climbed the hills. It took a long, long time. Maybe a week. There was lots and lots of snow. It was all white and shiny and cold.

Mr. Ted thought maybe there would be penguins. They got to hear a growl outside. It was a snow monster. It was all big and scary. He got big giant claws that was all black. He got sharp teeth too and was going to eat everyone all up.

Mr. Ted and Stupid Boy got their swords and went outside to chop the monster up. Mr. Ted hit the monster with his sword and the monster cried.

Stupid Boy feeled sad in his tummy. The snow monster was cold. He wanted to sit in the tent by the fire.

They all got to be friends.

The End.

It takes a long time to drive to the hill part in the lakes. We have to go past the normal place. But we are going to a different part. There is a big car park though. It is made of stones and things. The car sounds all funny when it goes over them. There is a path and some signs and they have lots of funny names. They say we have to go up the hill. It is something called Tarnhouse.

There are lots of danger signs too. They have pictures of big giant cliffs on them because the paths have big parts to fall down and it is a long, long way. Maybe if someone falls down there they will die.

Sheba gets to come with us too. I play with her. She likes to run backwards and forwards and chase the stick we found. She holds the stick in her mouth and it bashes on my legs. When I try to pull it out she doesn't let me. She is very strong and good at tug of war. When I get it, she wags her tail so I get to throw it again.

My mum tells me to stop it. She says I am getting on her nerves. I ask my dad if I can play in the bushes part of the path. He says yes. They have to get the things out of the car. Then my dad gets a special bag on his back so we can walk and he can carry everything.

They get a buggy for my brother. He is like a big baby. He doesn't be able to walk all the way up the hill. My mum says he will get too tired about it and he is only little. But they don't be able to carry him.

We walk up millions of paths. There is a wall. It is made out of stones. Big black and grey stones. My dad says that trolls made it and then people don't be able to run away. Then the trolls get to eat them all up because they catch them. I push the stone at the top of the wall. It falls down and rolls away. It makes a crash and a bash noise when it hits lots of rocks. My dad says it is bad to do that. I will get in trouble for destroying things. So I have to stop it.

It takes forever to get to the top. Maybe all week. Me and Sheba are all tired. She pants and has her tongue hanging out at the side. There is a stream that comes down the hill. She drinks in that and I make splashes. My dad says I will ruin my walking boots. But it is lots of fun.

At the top of the hill there is a big giant lake. It is like the lake that we went to before. But there isn't an island at the other side. It doesn't have another side. Maybe it falls off the hill. Maybe it is the edge of the world.

It is quiet. No one comes here. We get the lake just to ourselves. It is very nice. Maybe it is a secret place. Maybe they are just all lazy bones and they don't want to walk up the big hill. I like walking up the hill. It is lots of fun with Sheba. We get to have an adventure. We can tell Mr. Ted about it when we get home. He wasn't allowed to come because he will get wet and dirty. Maybe me and Sheba can jump off the top of the hill like Superman. Then we can tell Mr. Ted.

There are lots of big giant rocks in the water. They are sticking out. Sheba walks in the water and I walk on the rocks. My dad does it too. He jumps on a big giant rock. He makes a monster noise. He says he is going to catch me. He says he is going to get me and throw me in the lake. Me and Sheba run away very fast. My dad is silly.

J D STOCKHOLM

My dad jumps onto the next rock and he is laughing about it. Me and Sheba try to get far away. But there aren't more rocks and then it is the lake. My dad has big feet. He gets his boot stuck. He falls over and falls off the rock. There is a big giant splash. He says lots of swear words about it. I don't be able to keep the laughing away. My mum laughs about it too. I think Sheba gets to laugh about it. My mum sits with my brother. They are on a blanket on the grass. She is sunbathing. She doesn't have any top on. She doesn't get up to see if my dad is okay.

Me and Sheba go to see if he is okay. His hand is bleeding. He has made his little finger all sore. There is lots of blood too. Maybe all his blood will come out. My dad shows me his finger. I look at it. My dad is all sneaky. He gets me in his big arms. He lifts me all the way up in the sky. I scream at him to put me down. I keep laughing and so does my dad. He has tricked me. He is a big fat liar. Sheba barks at him too. She tells him to put me down. But he doesn't. He walks into the water and I make my arms get his neck. But he is big and strong and he throws me in the lake. It is all cold and Sheba comes too.

My dad thinks it is very funny. Me and Sheba go to my dad. I try to make my face have the angry eyes. But I don't be able to because my mouth keeps smiling and I keep laughing. I sneak up on my dad. Maybe we can trick him too. I jump on him and I make him all wet. But he is big. I don't be able to make him fall over and land in the water again. He gets my arms and legs and he is going to throw me again. I hug my arms on his neck and keep laughing when I say, "No, no."

My dad says he is going to get dry. Me and Sheba can go and play in the water. She likes to swim. She likes her stick and I throw it. She jumps in the water and goes to get it. Then she gives it back to me and I throw it again. We play lots of games.

My mum and dad sunbathe. My brother is tired and he falls to sleep in his buggy. There doesn't be anyone around. My mum and dad don't wear any clothes to sunbathe. They lie there until it is time to get food. Then my mum shouts and tells me to take my wet clothes off. I have to sit there in a big towel. I shiver because it is all cold and makes my teeth want to bash together.

We eat all the picnic. There is lots of it. I like the chicken that my mum makes. It is all spicy and crispy. My dad lies down when he finishes. He flicks my mum on her nose. She slaps him on the arm. They have a silly play fight and they laugh about it. My dad gets my mum's hand and he put it on his thing. She laughs and then she takes it off. I don't look. Me and Sheba sit and we keep eating the food.

My mum gets a pen and draws on my dad's tummy. My dad tries to get the pen off her. She gets his arms and holds him down. She tells me to come over and get him for her.

She tells me to draw flowers on his tummy. I do and then I draw a scary face. My dad tries to get away. But my mum holds him there and he doesn't be able to. I draw all over him. My mum gets my hand with the pen. She tells me to draw on this thing. I don't want to. She says it is okay. I am scared about it. Maybe I will make it hurt like the nail varnish.

My dad gives up. We are too strong for him and he has lots of pictures all over. My mum lets him go. She gets some real flowers. The white and yellow ones that are called daisies. She gets me to chop the end off. Then it is sharp. My mum holds my dad's thing and she tells me to put the flower inside. I don't want to but my mum laughs about it and tells me to do it. My dad doesn't shout. Maybe it will hurt. But he keeps saying my mum's name to stop it. She laughs.

She tells me to hold my dad's thing with the flowers sticking out. She tells my dad he isn't allowed to move. He will be in lots of trouble. She gets his sore finger and she bends it. She laughs about it. Then she gets her camera and tells me to smile. I hold his thing and smile. She takes pictures of me. She says I have to smile all big about it.

STUPID BOY

TWENTY TWO

One day, Stupid Boy was walking down the mountain. He said goodbye to the snow monster.
It was dark and Stupid Boy wasn't able to see. He tripped over a rock. He fell down the mountain and bashed his head. All his brains falled out.
Then Stupid Boy died.

The End.

We stay at the lake all day long. We stay there until the sun decides it is time to get ready for bed. It gets cold too. We have to walk all the way down the hill again. We have to be careful because there are rocks and we don't want to trip and fall over. My brother sits in his buggy. He is tired. My dad pushes him because my mum is tired too. My dad carries the things on his back.

Sheba walks with my mum. She is tired too. She walks very slow down the hill with my mum and dad. My mum and dad don't talk to me. They don't talk to me all day. After the flowers. Maybe I am bad. They don't shout at me. They don't say bad words. I ask them if we are going home but my dad doesn't say anything at all. Maybe he doesn't hear me.

Maybe my badness got out and I don't know about it. I walk next to my mum. I tell her it is a nice day.

"Get out of my sight," she says.

I walk behind them. Then they don't get to see me.

I am bad. My mum wishes I go away. She tells my dad that I am a pain. He says it is okay because I am going back to my Nan's the next day. I don't cry about it. I am bad. I feel all the bad inside. It makes my dad do the hurt thing in the morning. I am a stupid bad ugly boy and I wish I could go away forever. Maybe I can fall down the hill. Then I can die and my mum won't feel bad anymore. Maybe she can chop my head off because I am all bad. Then all the badness will come out and she can wish it all away.

It is nearly dark time. It takes a long time to walk down the hill. I walk by myself so my mum doesn't get more mad about it. I watch my feet when they walk. I don't trip over. I don't fall and bash my head open. I walk very slow then my mum and dad get to be far away. Maybe they will drive away without me. Maybe they will forget I am there and I will live at the hill.

I don't have Mr. Ted. I wish I did. We can stay at the hill and live there forever. But I have left him in bed. Andrew doesn't be with me either. I don't know where he is. He thinks I am bad because of the flower thing. He went away and now he doesn't come back. Everyone knows I am bad. I am stinky and bad.

My mum and dad don't talk to me when we are in the car. We don't get home. We go to a town place. It has lots of shops and boats and lots of nice things. My brother gets to walk. My mum and dad go in all the shops. I stay outside. I don't get anything. They don't want me to go in. Me and Sheba stand at the walls. She doesn't be allowed in because she is a dog.

My mum and dad go to the fish and chip shop. They get lots of food. I don't get any. My brother gets some chips. He eats them with the red tomato sauce. But he doesn't want them all. I wish I could eat them. They smell nice. I can smell all the hot vinegar. They make my mouth feel hungry. I don't ask my dad. He will shout and then I will be in trouble for my badness.

We walk on one side of the road and then we walk all down the other side when we come back. We look at the shops. I don't be allowed anything. My dad says everything cost lots of money. They don't have lots to spend. My dad has to work all the hours God sends. He says and then he doesn't have money because my mum spends it all. They buy my brother a plane. It is maked out of funny paper. My dad says it is cheap.

My brother doesn't know how to put it together. It has lots of little bits. I tell my brother I can do it. There is a picture on the back about how it looks. He sits outside with me and Sheba and my mum and dad go to look in the shop. I make the plane for him. Then he throws it and it flies. He runs after it. He lets me have a go too. It is lots of fun.

My mum and dad come out of the shop. I throw the plane and it nearly hits my dad. My dad picks it up and then he asks what I am doing. I tell him I am playing with my brother. He says I don't be allowed to play with his things.

"You'll break them," he says.

We walk some more around all the shops and then we get to go home. I sit in the back of the car with my brother and Sheba. Sheba gets on the floor because she is stinky and wet. I am very tired. I fall to sleep. Sheba and my brother fall to sleep too. We get to sleep all the way home.

I don't know that we have got back to my mum and dad's. I wake up and there is no one in the car. It is dark and I am still in the car.

I am all cold. My clothes are still a little bit wet. Because I have got to swim with Sheba. They make me do the shake thing. I get the goose bumps all over and my teeth try to bash together. It is dark all over. I am in the garden at my mum and dad's house. I can see all the bushes and the dark places.

My brain gets to think about the pictures. It thinks about the church people and all the dark. Maybe there is a man in the trees. He is going to come and get me. He will chase me around the house and I don't get to my mum. Then he will tie me on a table and make it all hurt. I hug myself all tight. I get scared about it. I don't like the pictures. There is lots of blood in them.

I look in the window. There is a light at the lounge. My mum and dad are sitting there. They are on the sofa and they are laughing about things and smiling. Maybe they don't be mad at me anymore. I wish I was in there. Maybe I can close my eyes and wish about it. Maybe I can make myself be in there too. Maybe they will get happy I am there. I wish my brain will keep the pictures away. I keep getting the picture about the man in the funny clothes.

I am scared in my tummy. I get out of the car. Then I run very fast to the house. I get to feel the man. Maybe he is like the bad man. I feel him behind me. I run very fast so he doesn't get me. I get the back door open. I close it very fast then he doesn't come. I feel it all at my back. My dad shouts at me and tells me not to slam the door.

I get to the lounge and my mum and dad is watching television. Maybe they don't know that I have come in. They don't say anything. They don't laugh anymore. Maybe they wish I would go away. I ask my dad if it is bedtime. But he doesn't tell me. Maybe I have been very bad at the lake place in the hill. They don't talk to me all the time.

I say night-night to them. I go upstairs. My brother is asleep in bed. I get my pyjamas on. I don't know if I have to put my clothes in the dirty washing. I make them in a pile for tomorrow. Then I get in my sleeping bag on the sun chair. I don't like the tears when that go down the side of my face and make it wet. Maybe my mum is fed up with me. I wish I don't get to wake up again when I go to sleep.

TWENTY THREE

Stupid Boy's dad was baking a pie. Like the ones in the song.

"Sing a song of sixpence, a pocket full of rye,
Four and twenty blackbirds, baked in a pie."

Stupid Boy thought it was very mean to bake birds in a pie. Maybe they didn't like it all hot and then it burned. They didn't get to die. That made Stupid Boy happy. When the pie got opened the birds began to sing. It was a dainty dish, to set before the king.

Stupid Boy didn't want to bake the birds though. So him and Mr. Ted got their swords. They scared everyone away. Then they opened the pie and let all the birds out. The birds was so happy they picked up Stupid Boy and Mr. Ted. Then they flied them all high up in the sky.

The king wasn't very happy. Now he had no dinner.

The End.

My dad likes to get funny things from the butcher to eat on Saturdays. The butcher is near his work. He is in the kitchen. He has a newspaper and it has lots of feathers on it. I stand next to him. I don't know what he is doing. He says he is making pigeon pie. I say he is being silly. My dad always says silly things.

STUPID BOY

My dad says it is true. He shows me. There are pigeons. He has some dead ones. He puts one in my hand. It is dead and hard. It is all cold from being in the fridge. I poke it with my finger. It is like a toy. Not like people or cats. They get to be squishy. I want to make the wings move about. But maybe they will snap off and then the dead bird will have broken wings.

I look at the pigeon. His eyes are open. They are all black and don't move. I pull one of the feathers and it pops out. I hope it doesn't hurt the pigeon. It hurts when my hair gets pulled out. My dad says not like that. He gets a clump of them and then he pulls them out. He says I have to do it the same way. That is how it is done properly. I do. It is hard to get them out. They make a pop and rip sound. Like cereal. My dad says all the feathers have to come out. Maybe the pigeon will get cold.

I pull all the feathers out. They all rip. I put them on the newspaper like my dad says. My mum comes into the kitchen. She wants some coffee. I hold up my pigeon. He is bald. He looks funny. I show her.

"That's disgusting," she says.

I put the disgusting pigeon down. She tells my dad she doesn't want to eat it.

Eat it?

I don't know my dad is going to eat it. They don't eat the blackbirds in the pie. Pigeons don't get eaten. My dad says they do. He says they taste very good.

Me and my dad get all the feathers out of all the birds. He asks me if I want to cut their head off and pull out their guts. I don't. I shake my head. My dad thinks it is funny. He laughs about it. My dad lets me go and play outside. It is a nice day. I get to play with Andrew.

There is a chicken in the garden. They come in lots of times. They get lost. Or maybe they are running away so they don't get eaten too. Andrew says maybe we can catch it. Not to eat it. We don't want to put it in a pie. We just want to get it.

Me and Andrew have very quiet shoes. They are bouncy and don't make any noise. My Nan bought mine. They are all new and nice and white. They make me jump very high. And they make me quiet so the chicken doesn't hear me. Sheba wants to help. Me and Andrew say no. She makes lots of noise.

Me and Andrew sneak around the big bricks. The chicken is going to walk to the gates. We get there too. We have a secret way and the chicken doesn't know about it. We hide behind the gate and she doesn't know. Then she gets there and we get out and grab her. She makes lots of noise. She gets to jump. I hold on very tight and take her to the house.

I put her on the floor in the kitchen. I show my dad. She doesn't make any more noise. Maybe she doesn't like to be hugged. He doesn't put the chicken in the pie. He has his pies in the oven with the pigeons. He looks at the chicken and he tells me to shush. Then he picks her up. She doesn't make lots of noise when he holds her.

My dad sneaks with the chicken through the dining room. And then he gets to the lounge but he doesn't go in. He makes the door open a little bit and then he lets the chicken go. We run away. I keep laughing. But I have to make it quiet or my mum will know about it. It is hard. Me and my dad run outside and we play with Sheba.

My mum screams. It is all big and loud. She gets her scared face on. She runs outside and shouts at my dad that there is a chicken. He doesn't be able to stop laughing about it. She doesn't know that we did it. I laugh because it is a trick.

"Go and get on your bike," she says to me and tells me to go away.

My dad goes to catch the chicken.

The pigeon pie is nice. We eat it for dinner in the evening time. My mum doesn't have any. She says she doesn't like it. She asks my dad why he gave me some. My dad says so I get to try it. She tells him he shouldn't and he isn't allowed to any more. My dad has given me a glass of his special drink too. She tells him he isn't allowed to give me the whiskey either. It makes me spoilt and it isn't fair on my brother when I get the good things.

My mum finishes her dinner. Then she gets up and goes to the sides. She doesn't have my cow cup. The one with no cow on it. But she gets another cup. She says I have to have some medicine. My evilness is getting out again. I don't want it. I don't want to get the sick out.

My dad tells me to go to the bedroom and stay there. I am sorry. I didn't mean to be bad again.

TWENTY FOUR

Stupid Boy got a new toy. He got it from Mr. Ted. It was a camera. He liked it very much. He got to take lots and lots of pictures with it.

He took pictures of flowers and trees. He took pictures of the sun and the sky.

Mr Ted thought it would be a good idea to take pictures of monsters. They could use it and get monster hunting. Stupid Boy thought it was a good idea too.

They got on some capes and their swords. Then they got their camera and sneaked about. The curtain monster was first.

They creeped all up the stairs.

Curtain monster didn't be there.

But he was sneaky. He was hiding under the bed. He jumped out and grabbed Stupid Boy and then he ate him all up.

The End.

I go to the bedroom. It is dark. I put the light on and hold my breath. Maybe the light doesn't go on and then the bad man is waiting in the dark. He gets to hear the light go click and then he knows I am there. Then he gets to jump out and get me.

He isn't there. The light turns on. I feel scared in my tummy about it. I creep to the other side of the room. Maybe he is hiding at the other side of my mum and dad's bed. But he doesn't be there. Maybe he is under the bed. I look. There is no bad man there. I look in the wardrobe too. My brain gets pictures about it. His big ugly pointy face and then he will get me.

It makes me shake inside. My tummy doesn't feel very good. It jumps about. But I am not going to get the sick out. I know he is in the room. I know he is going to come. I have been bad and I don't know about it. My mum is mad because I did something wrong. I get to feel it on my skin. The bad man is going to come and bite and scratch me. It hurts very bad when he does that.

My pyjamas are on my bed. I stand at the wall and then he doesn't be able to sneak up on me. I get my pyjamas on and then I get in bed. I am too scared to turn the light off. Maybe then the bad man will come out. He gets to be invisible.

My dad stands at the door. He smiles at me. I think I have been bad. But he smiles. Maybe I don't be bad. My mum is there too. She doesn't smile. But she doesn't have her angry face.

My dad asks me if I want to sleep in their bed. I like sleeping in their bed. Then I get to go to sleep and the bad man doesn't get his hands at the side of the bed. He doesn't get to grab me and hurt me. I tell my dad yes please.

It is cold in their bed. It makes me shiver. My mum makes the covers all tight and it is hard to get them open. My dad gets undressed. He gets in bed too. I ask him if it is his bedtime and he says it is. My dad hugs me. I close my eyes. My mum doesn't get in bed yet. She is looking for something in the bedside table.

My dad rolls me on my back. He makes my pyjama top all open. He gets his hands on my tummy. My tummy feels funny inside. I get my pyjama top and close the buttons. But my dad tells me to sit up and then he takes it off me. He throws it on my bed. He takes my pants off too.

He tells me to lie on my tummy. He hugs me again. My mum is there too. She is kneeling on the floor and the covers get off. I am cold. I hide my face in the pillow. Then my mum and dad don't know about my badness.

It makes my dad do the hurt thing. My mum gets to see it. I keep my eyes closed so she doesn't know about it. My mum tells me to look at her. But I don't want to. She will get to know I am all bad inside. She gets her hand and then she pulls my face. She tells me to open my eyes.

They want to cry. I don't blink. Because then the tears will all get out and go on the bed. My mum smiles at me. Maybe she doesn't know about the hurt thing.

My dad squashes on the bed. He is big and heavy and I don't be able to breathe. I try to keep it all in. My mum has got her camera. She is getting pictures of the hurt part.

My dad makes all his funny noises then he stops squashing me. I try to lie on my side and curl up. But my dad tells me to lie on my back. He gets his hands on my thing and then my mum is at the bottom of the bed. She takes pictures too.

I think inside my brain. In the morning I am going to play with Mr. Ted. We are going to hunt all the bad people. We are going to go on our bikes and ride very far. Maybe we can go to the house with the big gates where they keep the good people.

I like it when I get to be Andrew. He feels good inside. I get off the bed in my brain and I walk outside. Andrew leaves the Stupid Boy on the bed with his badness. We don't look at him. He is all bad.

We get to the house with the big gates and we are so big and strong that we snap them open. The bad people don't be able to beat us. We are strong. We get to hit them and scare them away and they don't come back.

My dad tells me to go and get dressed and clean up. I don't know I have gone to sleep. I feel like Andrew. Not Stupid Boy. But my dad is there. He talks and I get to be Stupid Boy again. With my badness.

I feel my badness all inside again. It is big and fat and ugly. I wish I get my mum's medicine and then I can get all the sick out. I get my pyjamas on. They are dirty on me. I make them all dirty and slimy. I wish I could take it all off and throw it away.

In the bathroom there is the ugly boy in the mirror. I screw my face up at him. I tell him I hate him. I say the hate word lots of times. I make the T very loud in my mouth. I keep saying it. But the T doesn't make the scratchy feel and then it doesn't make the badness go away.

I get my dad's razor and make it hurt on his stupid face. He doesn't get to cry about it. I tell him no. I say bad words like my mum and dad do. It is his badness that makes it all bad.

It gets to sting under his eye.

Good.

I am glad.

I am happy it gets to hurt.

Stupid Boy forever.

TWENTY FIVE

Stupid Boy got to drive his truck. He drived it with Mr. Ted, Sheba and Andrew. He didn't be a very good driver though. He drived it very fast and then it went off the cliff and falled all the way down. Then it crashed and they all set on fire.
Because Stupid Boy was stupid.

The End.

My dad says I can play with my truck tent downstairs. But I don't be allowed to make a mess. That makes my mum mad. Then she shouts lots of times because she has to clean more and more.

"And you know what she is like when she gets mad," my dad says and he does the eye thing.

Maybe they will fall away inside his head when he makes them roll back. I try to make my eyes roll away. But I don't be able to. I don't even be able to make them cross-eyed. My Nan says I got to follow my finger. I do it. But my eyes don't ever go across. My Nan can do it. She puts her pretend teeth out and makes her eyes cross. Mr. Ted can't do it either.

Me and Mr. Ted try to make Sheba do it. But she doesn't look at my finger. I get Mr. Ted and make him do it. But then she tries to bite him.

I pull Mr. Ted away all fast. Then she doesn't eat him. I get him away fast like Superman. Then I put my finger at her.

STUPID BOY

I tell her no. "No Sheba, you don't ever, ever bite Mr. Ted."

Sometimes, my brother plays in the truck with me. We put it under the stairs. We get torches. My dad lets me use his big one. Then we go hunting. We have to save Mr. Ted. Maybe Sheba bites him.

I sit inside and read my books. Then I don't get under my mum's god damn feet all the time. She doesn't like it when I do that. I do it lots of times and she gets mad about it. I always make my mum mad.

My dad says I can read my library books. I get them when I am good. My dad lets me get six from the library. Not four. I only get them if my badness doesn't get out. I try my bestest. Then me and Mr. Ted lie inside and read.

My mum is washing the dishes up. I sit in my truck because I have been good. I have my dad's torch. But it doesn't be dark yet. I like it. Mr. Ted likes it too.

My dad opens the door. He doesn't have his mean face.

"What are you doing?" He asks.

I show him my book. It is about ghosts and monsters.

My dad is big. Too big for my truck. But he comes inside. Then he has to sit on his knees. Maybe if he stands up the truck will go up in the sky.

"Can I see your book?" My dad asks me.

I nod my head all big and give it to him. He makes it closed and puts it on the floor.

"I have a surprise for you," he says to me.

Maybe it is a new book. I don't get lots of surprises. Only good boys get them. I have lots too much badness.

My dad lifts my top. He says I have to take it off. I let him pull it off my head. He takes my pants off too. I hug my knees all tight. Then my dad doesn't see my badness. I feel it all inside. Maybe it is like a monster in my book. It is big and bad. Maybe it is blue and hairy like monsters.

My dad has a skipping rope. I wonder if this is the surprise. It is like the ones the girls have at school. They do all their stupid skipping. With their stupid songs and stupid games. Girls are stupid sometimes. It is boring to skip. Sometimes I run through the rope when they are skipping. Then it doesn't be boring. They shout at me. It makes me laugh in my tummy about it. They have all big mad eyes and shout very bad and tell me off. They don't use the bad words though. I tell Mr. Ted about it. He says it is funny. I do it lots of times.

My dad tells me to put my hands out. He ties them all together. Like robbers. But I don't be a robber. I don't ever rob anything. My dad tells me to turn around and then I put my hands on my toy box. I hear his pants get open. It makes my tummy do the jumping thing.

He pulls me so I have to sit on his knee. He starts to do the hurt thing. He hugs me all tight and he whispers in my ear and tells me I will like it. He gets his hand and he puts it on my thing like I sometimes do to him. I keep the crying in my eyes. I don't let him know about it. I don't let it get out.

Mr. Ted is lying on the floor. I don't want him to look at me too. I tell him to go away in my brain, but he doesn't.

My dad says lots of words in my ear. He whispers and tells me that I am a good boy. I wish I got to go away.

My dad makes it feel funny inside. My mouth wants to make the funny noise like he does. I make my mouth closed all tight. Then my dad doesn't know that I like it. I am not allowed to like the badness. Then my mum will have to give me more medicine. Then I get the sick out and I don't like it. I don't like the sick in my tummy. It makes me scared inside.

My dad says I am being good. He says it lots of times. But I don't be. I am bad inside. Big and bad and stupid. My dad hugs me tight. His hand makes it feel funny and nice inside. It makes me let my breath out. My dad makes all the growl sounds too.

He lets me get off his knee. Then he gets my hands open. I don't want to look at my dad. I am sorry. I don't mean to be bad. It just comes out. Then all the bad things happen. I ask my dad if I can go upstairs. He says yes.

Maybe the bad man can get me. He gets me when I am bad. I go to the bedroom that is mine. I close the door. There doesn't be a bed. I sit on the floor. I put the music on then my dad doesn't hear me cry like a big baby. I get a cushion and I put it on my face. I scream my loudest. It makes my throat all scratchy inside. I do it lots of times. Maybe my head will explode. Then my brain is all out on the floor. I put my hands in my hair and pull it all tight.

I don't move forever and ever. It gets to dark time. My mum shouts I have to go to bed.

TWENTY SIX

Stupid Boy got stripy clothes. That was because he was a big fat robber. He tried to get away, but the lady monster catched him. She got some ropes and she tied them on his arms. She made them so tight that his hands nearly chopped off. Stupid Boy promised he would never ever be a robber again.

The End.

My mum laughs. We talk about Batman. Not the real Batman. The nice doctor with the big fast car. I have to go and see him. I have something on my foot. He is going to make it go away. Mr. Ted says it is a black spot. I showed it to him. My feet don't be bendy. I don't be able to see it properly. Maybe it is like pirates. They get black spots. But they put them on pirate hands. Maybe I am an upside down pirate. Then I have to walk on my hands.

I try to walk on my hands. But I always fall over. Stupid girls get to do it. Then they get the handstands at the wall at school. I tell them there is a spider on the wall. Then they scream and fall over. Girls always scream about everything.

I ask Mr. Ted if it is a pirate black spot. But he doesn't know. I show Sheba, but then she sniffs my foot and tries to lick it. But it tickles and I tell her to stop it. Andrew thinks maybe the pirates will come at night time. Then I can be a real pirate.

Pirates get black spots when they are mean and big bad robbers. They steal all the treasure and then they hide it under the big X place. Then the other pirates can find it and keep it. I don't be mean, but I do steal treasure. It's a secret. I don't tell Mr. Ted about it. He doesn't like robbers. Me and Peter do it.

My mum is excited in her tummy. Because we are going to see Batman. Maybe he will give her a big kiss. But I don't tell my dad about it.

"Do you think he will like my new skirt?" She asks me.

I think he will. Mr. Ted says yes too. My mum is very nice.

"I think he will say it is pretty," I tell her.

It makes her happy about it and she gets the silly smiley face on.

I hug Mr. Ted. We are happy about it too. We like to go to the doctor. He is very nice. My mum stands up. She looks at herself in the mirror. She turns around lots of times.

"All he wants is sex," my mum says. "That's all men want."

She gets her mad face about it. She says lots of bad words about the doctor. She says the doctor will have sex with all his patients.

"You're a boy. You're just as bad as they are," she says.

But I don't be.

I tell Mr. Ted when we are all big and lots of grown up then we won't ever do the sex thing. It makes people mad. My dad gets mad about it. He shouts at me sometimes when he does it with my mum. He says bad words and tells me to go away.

Sometimes it doesn't make my dad mad. Then he tells me to sit on the bed and they do the sex thing. But I don't like to see. It makes my tummy feel funny. Mr. Ted doesn't look too. Andrew tells me when I can open my eyes again. My dad says when I am big and grown up then I will like sex. He says it is very nice. Then he puts his finger in his mouth. I wish Mr. Ted and Andrew didn't get to see my dad do that. Then they know I do bad things.

"Close your eyes," my mum says.

Maybe she has a surprise for me. I ask Mr. Ted about it in my brain, but he doesn't know.

I make my eyes closed. My mum puts something on my head. I am a real pirate. But she puts it over my eyes and I don't be able to see. My mum laughs about it. Me and Mr. Ted do too. Maybe we are invisible.

My mum gets my hands. Then she ties them up like my dad does sometimes. But she does it behind my back. Like a real robber. But she doesn't make my hands get chopped off.

My mum gets her finger. It is cold and bony like a skeleton. She just puts it in the top of my pants and makes them get down. She laughs because I don't be able to get them back up. I laugh about it too. But I don't like it.

My mum goes away. I hear the door. It doesn't make a pop sound like my Nan's does. It makes a bang. I try and get my pants up. I don't know my dad is in the room. He is all big and sneaky. Like the bad man. It makes my tummy do the turn thing. My dad gets his belt open. I hear it. Then I hear his pants.

My dad puts his hand on my thing. He does the hurt part too. He doesn't say any words about it. I make my mouth all closed then I don't get to make the growl sounds like my dad does. My dad doesn't know I am bad. It is a secret. I don't even tell Mr. Ted. He won't be my friend anymore if he got to know about it. I don't make all the breathing noises, either.

My dad does. And he gets to growl in my ear. Then he unties my hands. But he doesn't take the pirate thing off my eyes. He goes away. I hear my mum and dad laugh in the kitchen. I hug my knees all tight. My tummy hurts inside from the hurt thing. I tell Mr. Ted I am sorry I am so bad. I wish I could go away.

I don't mean to let my badness out.

I get my pants back up. I go to the bathroom. I make the door locked. Then I lean on the wall and stare at Stupid Boy.

He is in the mirror.

I hate him.

I hate Stupid Boy.

He is bad and ugly and stinky. I wish he got to go away forever. He makes it all bad.

STUPID BOY

He is bad, bad, bad.

I get my dad's razor. I make it go under Stupid Boy's eye.

Then it hurts him.

Good. It gets to hurt lots. I watch it. Stupid Boy doesn't cry.

"Stupid Boy," I say to him.

I say stupid lots of times and make the T and the D feel in my mouth.

I go to the mirror. Maybe I can make him scared. I put the tap on. It gets all hot. Then the smoke goes on the mirror. I wipe it away.

Stupid Boy doesn't get to hide.

I put my hand in the water. I keep it there for a long, long time.

Stupid Boy starts to cry.

TWENTY SEVEN

Stupid Boy was going on a special trip. He didn't be able to wait. He was very excited in his tummy. But he didn't know that it was a monster cave. He didn't take Mr. Ted. No one helped Stupid Boy.

The monsters ate him all up.

The End.

My mum and dad say I can go to a special place for the summer time. There are lots of fun things to do. Lots of other children will be there. I get to sleep there too. Like a big giant sleepover. I don't be able to wait.

I don't be allowed to tell lots of people about it.

"They'll think we're made of money," my mum says. "I don't want people knowing what we have and getting burgled."

I tell my mum I won't tell anyone. Not ever. I make a big promise and cross my heart and hope to die. Stick a needle in my eye.

I ask Mr. Ted about that. Maybe someone bad gets to come. Like the bad man. Then he sticks needles in my eyes for being a liar. But I don't be. I won't tell anyone about the fun place. It's a secret. I tell Mr. Ted and Sheba shush about it and they do.

I get to go on Thursdays. It is summer time so I don't have to go to school. I stay at my mum and dad's all summer long. My mum thinks I will be bored. So the church asked her if I wanted to go to the fun summer place, and she said yes. Then I don't get bored. My mum is very nice. My brother doesn't get to go though. He is too little.

I don't be allowed to take Mr. Ted or Sheba or Andrew. Andrew says he will keep care of Mr. Ted and Sheba. Then the bad man doesn't be mean to them and make them go away. Maybe Mr. Ted will get scared in his tummy all by himself. But he says he doesn't be. I tell Mr. Ted I will be back on Monday. Andrew says then we can all go and play lots of games. I am excited in my tummy about it.

We are meeting at the park. It is next to my school. But my school is all closed. Maybe there are ghosts inside. All the gates are locked. But ghosts can get through the gates. Maybe they live inside. I look at the windows, but I don't see any. Maybe they only come out at the night time. Kirsty says there is a ghost girl there. She didn't be a good girl and then they hanged her up. It made her neck snap into pieces, but she didn't get her head chopped off. Kirsty says that she walks around and gets the bad children. I didn't ever see her though.

I have to wait for the church people. They are getting me in the car and then they will take me to the place. It is called a play scheme. We have to be at the park when the little hand is on the eight and the big hand is on the six.

We are early though. The big hand didn't get to the six yet.

I stand with my mum and dad. My brother is tired. My dad has to hold him. I have my bag. It has my lunch inside. My mum made me a sandwich. It has cheese. My brother let me put his special ketchup on it. I don't be able to use it but he said he misses me. So then he said I can have some. I told him thank you. My Nan puts sauce on my sandwich. Sometimes, I squeeze it all out and then I lick it. My mum tells me to stop playing with my damn food.

"If you're not going to eat it, then there is nothing else," she says.

But I do eat it all up.

I have an apple too and some crisps and a drink. I don't ever get a packed lunch before from my mum.

My dad gets them to go to work.

My dad has his packed lunch in the car. My mum made it for him too. But he can't hold his lunch and my brother. My brother is a big lazy bones. He still has his pyjamas on. I don't. I got dressed. My brother wiggles lots of times and my dad tells him to stop it.

He wiggles about too much. My dad doesn't be able to hold him. My brother slides down. He falls on the ground and bangs his head. He cries very loud.

His head has blood on it. My dad picks him up and my mum is mad. She says lots of bad words at my dad about it.

STUPID BOY

The big white car comes. I don't care. I don't want to go. Maybe my brother will have to go to heaven when I am away and then I don't get to say goodbye. I don't want him to go to heaven.

My dad tells me to get in the car.

I tell him no.

My eyes start to cry about it. My mum pushes me to the car.

"Get in," she says.

I don't want to. My tummy feels sad inside. I tell Mr. Ted in my brain about it all. Maybe he gets to hear me.

My mum pushes me inside and closes the door. She walks to my dad and brother and the car drives away. I want it to stop. I don't want to go. But it doesn't.

I look at my mum and dad through the window. I wave at them. But they don't see it. They don't be waving. They walk to their car. My brother is crying. I make my mouth all tight then I don't let the tears out.

The car goes away and I don't be able to see them anymore. I look out the window. Maybe they will come in their car behind and make it stop and take me home. But they don't.

We go and get another boy and a girl. But I don't talk to them.

They look sad too. Maybe they have sad tummies because they have to leave their mum and dad's.

I hug my bag. I wish I had Mr. Ted.

TWENTY EIGHT

Stupid Boy went to the big bad house. With all the bad monsters. It is a trick and he didn't have Mr. Ted. No one got to hear him ever again. They put him inside and locked him in the jail. Then they chopped him into a million bits and throwed him all away.

The End.

We stand there and the man shuts the gate. They are big, giant, black gates. He gets a chain on them and a lock. My dad has chains and locks on his bikes sometimes, then maybe no one can steal them. Maybe someone wants to steal the gates.

There are spikes on the top.

"If anyone tries to climb over the gates, they will slip and the gates will get stuck in their bellies. They will have to stay on the gate forever," the man says.

I don't know why anyone will climb on them. They are very high.

We go in the house. It is a big white house but it doesn't have nice shiny windows. Not like lots of houses. It has a board. Maybe the window is smashed. Maybe that is why there gets to be a chain on the gate and a lock. They even have guard dogs. Big black dogs. They stand there with chains on their necks. But maybe they don't have locks in them.

STUPID BOY

The other two children follow the man in the house and then maybe I have to do the same. The house smells all bad. Like hot pee. It makes my tummy want to do the turn thing. It smells like cigarettes too and the beer my dad drinks from his tin cans.

I don't know what I am supposed to do. No one tells me and I don't want to be bad. Maybe my dad will come and shout at me about it.

There is another man there too. He takes my bag off me and throws it on a table. Then he takes my hand. The man takes me up the stairs. We get to go in a room that has a sofa and a table and a television. I don't ever know a house that has the lounge upstairs. The man tells me to sit down and wait there. I do. I have to be good. I wish I get Mr. Ted with me or Andrew or Sheba and then we can all sit and be very good and not get in any trouble.

There is another man. He is big and giant like my dad but he has funny hair with beads in and is very dark.

"Can I sit on the sofa?" He asks and I say yes.
 "Are you new here?"
I nod my head.

He asks me my name and I tell him. Then he sits back and I wait for the other man to come back. The dark man asks me what I have been doing this week and I tell him it is the school holidays and maybe I can get to play with my friends.

The dark man is nice. He has a big smile at me. He asks me what me and my friends do and I tell him we get to play games and things. I tell him about the card game that is called Pontoon. You have to make twenty one. My Nan told me how to play it and then me and my friends all get to do it.

The man says he don't ever play that.

"Can you teach me?" He asks.

There are some cards he says, and then he opens a cupboard. There are games and books and playing cards.

He asks what we use to bet and I tell him matches and then when we all run out, we get to use shoes and socks and things like that.

He says we don't have any matches but we can use our shoes and socks. I don't know if I am allowed to. Maybe the other man who told me to sit will get mad at me about it. But the dark man says it is okay. They take a long time to come back and if we get in trouble, he will say it is his fault.

He doesn't be very good at the game. He doesn't be able to beat me. I tell him lots of times how to do it but he doesn't get it right. He gets both his shoes and socks off.

Then I say I won because he doesn't have anything else. He says maybe he can win them back. But I win again. He says it is okay. He has a t-shirt and he takes that off instead.

He wants to play the game but I don't like it. He gets to sit there with just his underpants on. I tell him maybe I get to go now.

"We are just playing and you are a very good teacher," he says.

STUPID BOY

We play again but then maybe he gets good at it and I don't win. He tells me to take my shoes off. I lose lots of times. I don't want to play anymore but he keeps saying one more game and then I get there in just my underpants too.

And I don't like it when he gets to lose and he has no clothes at all. My eyes keep looking at his thing but I don't want to. He tells me to deal again. I do and then I lose. He tells me it is fair if I take all my clothes off too. I squeeze myself all tight then he doesn't get to look at me with no clothes on.

He keeps asking to play. I keep looking at the door. Maybe the other man will come back and then I don't have to play. The dark man loses again, but he doesn't have any clothes left.

"I have an idea," he says. "We can do nice things like friends do for each other."

He tells me to lie down on the sofa because he lost and he has to do the nice thing to me. He pushes me back so I lie down. I try to keep my hand over my thing so he doesn't see it but he tells me it is okay and he moves my hand away.

He puts his hand all on my tummy and my chest and my arms. Then he gets his mouth and puts that on my chest and tummy too. He gets his mouth near my thing and I shake my head. But he says it is okay and it is a nice thing. Then he does like I do with my dad and he puts his mouth there. It makes me feel all funny inside. I get my eyes closed so then the dark man doesn't see I am bad.

Then we play the cards again and he beats me. He says it is my turn to be nice. He says I should do what he did. I don't want to put his thing in my mouth, but he says then I will be cheating if I don't.

He does it like my dad and puts my head there. He smells and tastes all bad in my mouth, but he doesn't let my head get back up right away. I don't know he is going to do the yucky part too and it makes me all cough. I don't keep the crying away from my eyes. The dark man says he is sorry. He didn't know that was going to happen.

He gets my top and says to wipe my mouth with it. He says he feels very bad. He didn't mean for it to happen. He says my clothes are dirty now too and maybe the other man has a clean top I can use. He says he will go and get him.

The dark man goes away. He is going to find the other man. I sit there and hug myself all tight. Maybe I can go home soon. I feel it inside that I miss my mum. Maybe she wishes I am home too.

The dark man is a long time but he comes back with the other man. The dark man says he has told them about my card game and will I show the other man just one time. I shake my head because I am scared in my tummy. Maybe I will lose and get to do the yucky thing again.

The dark man says it is okay and the other man says he really wants to see it so he can learn how to play the game.

The dark man deals the cards out and tells me to pick mine up. I get good cards. I win. The dark man says I am just too good at it and I need another prize. I don't. I don't want one.

The dark man says it is fair and the other man says it is fair too. The dark man comes over to give me a big hug and then tells me to lean on the sofa. I don't know he is going to do the hurt thing. He gets his thing and he put it inside like my dad does. Then the other man gets to take a picture about it. I don't like it but the dark man holds my hands up and gets his face in mine. He makes it hurt lots of times.

TWENTY NINE

The monsters keeped Stupid Boy inside the dark house. They put chains on his hands and feet. They keeped him there forever. He didn't ever be able to get away. Maybe Mr. Ted could come and then he would chop Stupid Boy's hands and feet off and he could get away.

The End.

I wish I have Mr. Ted. I wish I can go home. I don't feel very well in my tummy. It is all bad inside. I don't like the play place. Lots of people do the hurt thing all day long. Then I have to be on pictures. It makes me sad; I don't be able to smile about it.

I lie in the room. There are lots of other boys and girls too. My tummy is all sore inside. I don't be able to keep the crying away. But I make it quiet then I don't get shouted at. We don't be allowed to cry. Then they shout at me and smack me until I make it go away again.

I hug my knees all up to my tummy. But it makes me cry more about it. Maybe they chopped me all up and I don't know about it. Maybe that's why I was bleeding. Then they made me clean it all up. My mum usually cleans it all away. She makes me stand in the bath or the bowl in the kitchen. But my mum isn't here. I have to do it all by myself.

STUPID BOY

But I don't be allowed to go in the bathroom by myself. They take pictures about that too.

It is dark time. The man said it is time to go to bed. We don't get any beds. We don't get a sun chair either. The man says we have to lie on the things on the floor. They are off a bed. The squishy part. They don't be very comfy. We have to share them because there is only three, but there are seven children. We all sleep like bears in the song. When the little bear said everyone had to roll over and then one falled out. We don't fall out though. We don't be bears. Maybe Mr. Ted would fall out if he got to sleep in the bed.

My hand is sore. I don't be able to hold the cover very tight. The girl next to me has too much and I don't be able to pull it back. The dark man made my hand all sore because he squished it down. He didn't mean to. He said he was sorry about it. I told him it was okay. I didn't want him to be sad about it.

Maybe the girl next to me is asleep. I don't ask her for more cover. We don't be allowed to talk. Maybe they will chop out my tongue if I say any words. She doesn't be talking either and she doesn't be crying. She hugs hers knees too. Maybe she has a Mr. Ted she misses too.

I don't need lots of cover. They are all stinky anyway. Maybe it is like my brother's coat when he sleeps with it lots of times. But I don't take it all the way off. It is cold.

There is someone coming. I get to hear their feet. They don't be like the bad man. The bad man is all sneaky.

They open the door. We all pretend to be asleep. I don't move. Like a statue. But there doesn't be any music. The man who taked the pictures comes in. He stands next to me. I keep my eyes all tight shut then he doesn't know I am awake. Like my dad doesn't know I am awake when he does the hurt thing and then he doesn't know that I am bad. Maybe I am invisible and he doesn't see me. Maybe my badness got out and I didn't know about it.

He doesn't shout at me. He kneels down and then pulls my cover off. The girl doesn't be awake. She doesn't move when it is gone. The man pulls my pants off too. I try to get my pants, but he doesn't let me. He smacks my hand very hard and then he smacks me in the face and I cry very bad about it. I wish my mum would come and get me, but she doesn't and the man takes all my clothes off. There is another man. He comes too. I don't be able to make them go away. I don't get to make it all stop. The man gets his thing at my mouth and the other man does the hurt thing. I try to cry very loud but they hit me and shout at me. No one comes. I wish I had my mum. I tell her in my brain lots of times to come and get me.

STUPID BOY

THIRTY

*Stupid Boy waked up. It was all nice and
sunny outside. The sun had got his hat on.*
Stupid Boy singed the song about it.
Hip, hip, hooray.
*The big bad people heard him sing it. They
didn't like the song. Stupid Boy singed all stupid and
stinky.*
*The people got Stupid Boy and put him in the
shower and washed him all away forever.*
The End.

It is morning time. It doesn't be nice
and sunny. The sun doesn't get his hat on.
He is sad in his tummy. He doesn't want to.
My hand is still sore too. Maybe it will fall off
into a million pieces. My eyes are all big and
giant. Maybe I get to look like a bug. A big
fat stupid bug that is all bad.

The man and his friend went away.
Maybe they went away because I falled to
sleep. I didn't know about it. It was on
surprise. The man's friend did the hurt thing
very bad and it made me fall to sleep.
Maybe I got to die but I didn't go to heaven.
It hurt like I got to die. But only good people
gets to go into heaven. God asks them if
they have been good. He is like Santa. He
knows if all the boys and girls have been
nice. I don't be good and nice. So he doesn't

let me be in heaven. Santa doesn't get me presents because I am bad too. I try not to cry about it. I try to be good lots of times. Maybe Santa and God will get to know I try my bestest.

The man comes to the room. He makes the door open and then he turns on the light. It is very bright. My eyes all set on fire. I look at the light. It is a bulb like my dad has in his garage. It hangs all by itself. My mum doesn't like them. They don't be nice and pretty. They make it all ugly and bad.

I like the moth things. They jump up and down on the bulbs at the night time. I like moths. My mum doesn't. She makes my dad catch them and squish them. She says moths eat clothes. I don't ever see moths eat clothes. I put a moth in my mum's drawer, but all the clothes was still there and they didn't be eaten. I think my mum is silly. Moths don't be able to eat clothes. They are all too small and the clothes are like big giants clothes.

Maybe giant moths can come and eat the man. Then he doesn't do the hurt thing again. My mum has moth balls. They don't look like balls of moths. Maybe the moths are very good at hide and seek. Maybe I can hide from the man in a ball like the moths do and then he doesn't ever find me and do any more bad things.

The man tells us to get out of bed. We are 'lazy little shits,' he says, and then he uses lots of bad words. They make my tummy do the turn upside down thing. He says it is breakfast time. But I don't be hungry in my tummy. It is all sore and it hurts very bad.

My tummy and my legs all have tummy aches inside them. I don't be able to walk very fast. But the man tells us we have to hurry up or there is lots of trouble.

We have porridge. But it isn't very nice. It is very runny with lots of big fat lumps in it. It doesn't have sugar on it. I eat it very fast though. Then I don't get in lots of trouble about it.

The man shouts at me. He calls the kitchen bad names and tells me to get my bowl in there. I have to swish it in the cold water and make it all clean. He tells me I have to get clean too. He tells me to go to the bathroom. He calls the bathroom lots of names too.

I have to wait for someone else to finish. I don't be allowed in the bathroom all by myself.

There is another boy. He is smaller than me. The man tells us to get in the shower. I don't want to get in together. But we have to. The boy gets the soap and then he tries to make me clean. But I want to do it. The man smacks my head.

"You clean him, he cleans you," he shouts at me.

I don't want to, but the man slaps my leg very hard and makes it sting. The crying gets out. The man tells me to do as I am told.

I do.

"Smile," he says.

Then he takes lots of pictures about it.

THIRTY ONE

Stupid Boy lived with the monster people. But not even the monster people liked him. He got lots of things wrong because he was the stupidest stupid boy ever in the whole world.

They hit him with their hands and maked him cry. They told him to go away lots of times, but he didn't be able to because the doors was all locked and he didn't know the way home. So they squished Stupid Boy into lots of bits.

The End.

I don't like the play scheme place. It is bad. I wish I got to go home. I miss Mr. Ted. I feel it in my tummy. I try to tell him in my brain that I miss him lots and lots, but he doesn't say anything. Maybe he doesn't hear me. Maybe he is mad because I have gone away and I didn't take him with me. Maybe he is glad I got away and then he doesn't have to see me ever again. Or, maybe he was sad and then he cried lots of times and then maybe he died and when I go home again Mr. Ted is all gone because he has gone to heaven. I won't ever see him again because I don't be able to go to heaven. I am too bad all inside. My mum told me I am. That is why the bad man comes at night-time. Maybe that is why the bad people don't make the play place very nice.

It is Monday, and the people say that we go home today. We have to go to the bathroom first. We have to be all nice and clean to go home. We don't be allowed to get in the shower alone. The man takes the pictures about it again. The man is mad at me. I didn't be bad. Not ever. I didn't shout and I didn't let my badness get out. But, the man is mad at everyone. Maybe the other children have badness inside like me. Maybe it is all inside like a big monster and then their mums and dads don't want them too. Like mine. My mum wishes I didn't ever be born. It is my dad's fault because he made her do the thing to get babies and she didn't want to.

The man gives me my clothes. I didn't bring any new clothes with me. I only had one pile of clothes. But I didn't wear them all weekend. The man had taked them away and keeped them safe. They didn't be dirty. My mum doesn't let me wear clothes that are dirty. Unless I get my badness out. Then I be too bad to wear nice, clean clothes. Sometimes, my dad doesn't let me get clean clothes. He says I am bad too.

We ride in the car again. We are going back to the park I think. I don't ask the man. He shouts lots of times. I don't look out the windows. I feel bad in my tummy. Maybe my tummy wants to cry. Not even the sun has his hat on because he is sad too. Everyone is sad. I don't be smiling inside. It went away. Maybe Mr. Ted has it.

STUPID BOY

We drive to the park. My dad is there. He is in his car. He is reading his book. He doesn't look at me. I get out of the car and then the man drives away. He drives away so fast he makes me nearly fall over. Like Superman flied passed all fast and then it went whoosh. But, I didn't fall over.

I go to my dad's car and then I open the door.

"Did you have a good time?" my dad asks me when I get in the car.

I don't say anything to him. I don't want to tell him about the place. Maybe he will be mad at me because I did lots of bad things. Maybe he will get mad because I let all the men do the hurt thing lots of times. I don't ever tell them no.

My dad doesn't shout at me because I don't say an answer. I think he will later. It is rude not to answer people when they ask a question. My dad says it is bad manners and I don't be allowed to have any bad manners because they are free. I didn't know you could buy them.

I don't say anything all the way to the house. I don't have words to say. They have all gone away. Maybe my brain went to sleep. It doesn't want to think about anything. My tummy hurts. It hurts on the inside and the outside. My arms all hurt too. My arms have lines on them because a man tied them up very hard and he didn't make them get untied when I cried about it. He told me to shut up. But, it hurt very bad and it started to bleed. All my blood didn't come out. But, they have a scab on them and I pick at them. I don't let my dad see. He doesn't like me picking at things.

We go to my mum and dad's house. We don't go to my Nan's house. It is summer time and I don't have school so I stay with my mum and dad all the time. My mum is in the kitchen. She is making food. My tummy has the sick inside. It doesn't want to eat any food. Maybe the sick will come out and I won't know about it. My mum will get mad at me. It makes me scared because if the sick comes out then she will shout at me. My dad will smack me for being bad and I don't be there very long. Maybe they will send me to the bad house again.

"Get in the bath," my mum says to me. "It is already run and there is a towel on the side. Don't make a mess or there will be trouble."

I tell her okay and then I go up the stairs. I don't like it up there all by myself. Maybe the bad man is hiding because I have been bad. I haven't seen the bad man for a lot of times. Maybe he doesn't know where my mum and dad's house is?

"And don't leave your stinking clothes lying around," my mum shouts up the stairs to me. I tell her I won't.

I go to the bathroom and then I close the door. I have to take my clothes off, but I don't want to. It makes my tummy feel sad and then my eyes want to cry about it. I stand at the door and then it can't get open and then my mum and dad can't see that I am stupid boy and I get the crying out like a big fat baby. I take my shoes off and my socks. It hurts to take my pants off because all the hurt things make it hurt very bad. My clothes have blood in the pants. I fold them so my mum doesn't see them. She will be mad because she has to wash it all away. I take my jumper off too and I make it in a nice neat pile. I don't put the socks in a ball. The pants and jumper and socks and underpants makes it four. So, I make the socks not in a ball and then there is two socks and it is five and then nothing bad can happen.

I get in the bath. The water is cold. Maybe my brother got to use it before me. It is grey and it doesn't have bubbles in it. My dad comes in and tells me he is going to wash my hair. I don't do it right.

"Your mother said I have to wash it to make sure all the greasy crap is out," he says and I nod my head and then I hug my knees all up.

My lips want to shake because I am cold and I get to shiver. My dad gets the cup and then he pours the bath water on my head. I try to make my back move away from it because it is too cold.

"Keep still," my dad says and then he grabs my head and makes it be in the right place. I don't cry about that. The tears is all gone and dried up. Maybe they dried up forever. I wonder if Andrew missed me too.

I know he is there, but I don't be able to see him. I can hear him. He is there. I close my eyes and

I know he can see me in the bath. I don't tell him about the bad people. Then he won't be my friend anymore because I am all bad inside. He tells me that he has looked after Mr. Ted and they played lots of games.

Andrew tells me about the game he and Mr. Ted played. It is lots of fun. He shows it me in my brain and Mr. Ted and Andrew get to be super spies. I get to be a special spy too. We have black clothes on and then no one can see us at night time because it makes us invisible. We go to the bad house on our bikes. I have a big giant motorbike like my dad and the bad people hear its growl noise and they get all scared. But they don't be able to run away because we are very good. We run them over.

I don't know that my dad has finished. He shouts at me and smacks the back of my head.

"Get out of your own world and into this one," he says to me. "If you keep making the clicking sound I am going to send you to the loony bin and you won't get out." I don't know I was making the clicking sound. I try not to do it, but my mouth likes it.

"Okay," I say to my dad and then I try and feel the 'k' in my mouth when I say the word, but I don't say it again because my dad will send me away. Sometimes I make it quiet and then he doesn't hear it.

STUPID BOY

"Go and get dressed now," my dad says. "There are clothes on your bed and don't wake your brother, he's not feeling well and he is in bed."

My dad makes the bathroom clean again and he lets the water out. He has to make the black ring on the side wash away or my mum gets sad about it, because she can't make it go away.

My clothes are on my camp bed. My dad comes in and he sits on his bed. My brother is asleep in there. I don't make any noise. My dad watches me get dressed and he smiles about it. He does the thing with his finger in his mouth. I don't look at him. It makes me feel more bad inside. Maybe my dad wants to do the hurt thing too.

My dad tells me to come to him. I do. I don't be finished getting dressed yet. He gets my hand and puts it on his thing. My tummy does the turn over thing. I don't want my dad to do the hurt part. It all stings inside from the people at the house. But he doesn't. He moves my hand until he makes the funny noise.

"Get dressed and come downstairs," he says to me.

Then he goes downstairs and leaves me in the bedroom. Maybe the bad man will come. I tell him to come and get me. I tell Andrew to tell the bad man I am all bad inside and he should make me go away forever.

I get on my knees and then I put my head on the floor and I hug my tummy and the crying wants to come out too hard. It makes me make a noise and maybe my head will go pop because the crying is too big. It makes my head hurt. I cry my hardest, but it doesn't go away. I get my fingers and then I make them dig into my arms and make it all hurt and cry all at the same time. I do it so much that the sick wants to come out and it gets on the floor.

STUPID BOY

THIRTY TWO

Stupid Boy was so stupid that his mum and dad didn't want him back anymore. They was so sick and tired of him that they throwed him away. It was monster day and the monster people got Stupid Boy. But he shouted about it and asked Mr. Ted to bring his sword so he could chop them all up, but Mr. Ted didn't because he decided Stupid Boy was bad too. So Stupid Boy ran away and then he falled off a cliff and died because he splatted on the rocks and the trolls ate him all up.

The End.

My mum wakes me up very early. I am a lazy bones because my brain is all sleepy. My brain stayed awake all night long. Then the sun came out and it went to sleep. Me and Mr. Ted stay awake so the bad man doesn't get to come. My eyes don't be closed when it is dark time because then the bad man comes when I am not looking and maybe he hurts Mr. Ted.

I don't like it when my mum and dad go to bed. Then they are sleeping and the bad man can come because then my mum and dad doesn't hear him. Me and Mr. Ted watch the door then he doesn't get inside and hide behind the curtains.

"Get dressed," my mum says to me.

She gives me my clothes. I don't know we are getting up early. Maybe we are going somewhere nice. She tells my brother to get up too. Then she gets his clothes. But she has to put them on him because he is a baby and can't do it himself. She gives him his baby bottle and he stands and drinks it. Then he hugs his stinky red coat all tight.

"Hurry up," she says to me.

I get dressed very fast. I run to the bathroom and use the toilet and then I have to brush my teeth. I get them finished before my mum goes down the stairs.

My mum has sandwiches on the table and a bag. Maybe we are going out all day long. It is Thursday. I don't know about going anywhere. My mum and dad didn't say about it. My mum has medicine on the side. I don't know that my badness has got out again. I don't want to take the medicine. It makes the sick come out and then my neck all hurts inside.

I don't make any sounds then maybe my mum will forget to give me the medicine. But, she doesn't. She mixes it up in a cup and then she comes to me.

"Open your mouth," she says. I shake my head. I don't want to.

"Are we going out?" I ask my mum.

"We are going to the Pleasure Beach," my dad says when he comes in the kitchen. "After we have dropped you off."

STUPID BOY

My mum puts the spoon at my mouth but I shake my head away. I tell my dad I want to go too. I can feel my badness inside.

My dad shakes his head about it. "You and your Nana go all the time; it's your brother's turn."

But, I want to go with them. I don't ever go with them before. I go with my Nan sometimes, but we don't go on lots of things because it costs lots of money. My mum doesn't like me going with my Nan. Me and my Nan keep it a secret lots of times.

I ask my dad one more time. I don't ask lots because that makes him mad. He says no. It's just for my brother not for me. I'm not invited.

My mum tells me to open my mouth, but I don't want to. I keep telling her no. I don't want the medicine to make the sick get out of my tummy. I ask my mum if I can take Mr. Ted.

"You're not going to your Nan's. We're dropping you off at that park."

My tummy does the turn over thing inside and my eyes get all wet. I don't want to go. I shake my head about it. My tummy gets all filled up inside and it makes me want to go to the toilet. I tell my mum I don't want to go there.

She asks me why. I shrug my shoulders. I don't want to tell her the bad things. She will know I am all bad inside. I don't want her to know about it. Then she will make me go away again.

I tell her I don't want to go. The words don't come out good because my eyes are all crying about it. I shout them at her and it makes her mad. She shouts back that I have to tell her why. I say I don't want to. Please don't make me go there.

"Take your medicine," she says and I shake my head about that too. She gets the spoon and then she squashes it at my mouth. I make my head get away so she can't. Then I put my hands over my mouth. My dad shouts too. He tells me to do as I am told. I tell them not to make me go to the play place.

"You're going," my dad says. "You're going to ruin our day." He calls me lots of bad names.

My tummy gets all bad inside and I don't be able to stop it. She smacks my arm, but my pants get wet because I need the toilet and I don't be able to keep it inside when my tummy is scared.

My mum is mad. She has her angry face on. She throws the spoon on the wall and it bangs and the medicine makes a mess.

"Look what you have done," she shouts at me. She points at the medicine. But, I didn't throw it away.

My dad bangs his cup down and it makes me jump. My brother jumps too and then he starts to cry. I make everyone be bad. Maybe I should go away forever.

"Upstairs, right now," my mum shouts at me.

She pushes me and I don't be able to walk very fast. She pushes me hard in my back to make me get up the stairs. We get to the top and I go to the bathroom. It is the wrong way. My mum grabs my arm.

"Bedroom," she says.

She tells me to take my pants off. She gets some new ones out. I put the old ones on my bed. My mum shouts very loud. She calls me bad words because they are wet and I put them on the bed. I didn't mean to. It was on accident. I tell my mum I am sorry. I didn't mean to make my mum get lots more cleaning.

"Why can't you behave?" she asks me.

I tell her I am sorry. I won't ever do it again. I tell her I don't want to go to the play place. Please don't let me go. I promise to be good forever. I won't ever do anything bad. I say please lots of times. My crying makes me get the hiccups.

She tells me to stop being stupid.

I run to the door and then I stand by it so she can't make it open.

"Please don't make me go."

My mum tries to move me. But I be strong and I don't get out of the way.

"Move," she says.

I shake my head. She smacks me very hard on my leg. I don't get my pants on yet and it stings. I rub my leg. "Please can I stay here?"

She grabs my arm and digs her fingers all in. She slaps my leg lots of times like lots of fireworks banging. It is all red. I cry very loud.

I make myself be a ball on the floor. I hug my leg.

J D STOCKHOLM

"Please let me stay here."

STUPID BOY

Stupid Boy had to go to the monster people again. He went every weekend. He didn't like it there. Mr. Ted and Sheba didn't be there and he didn't get to take his sword and be able to chop them into lots of bits. The monster people didn't like Stupid Boy because he was so stupid. They got the police things and then put them on his hands so he didn't get away when the monster people wanted to hurt him.

Stupid Boy got his birthday. He didn't go to the circus with the nice lady. No one came and got Stupid Boy. No one sang Happy Birthday. The monster people just hurt Stupid Boy until he cried.

Stupid Boy got to be eight. He wished that his mum would come and get him and then she said happy birthday. But she didn't. Maybe she forgot. Stupid Boy cried very hard. Maybe she got to hear him if he cried lots of times. But she didn't. There didn't be any presents or any cake. They forgot it was his birthday.

The End.

I don't like the play place. I wish I don't have to go there anymore. I go there on the weekends when I don't go to school for the holidays. I stay at my mum and dad's too. But they don't like me there. I make too much noise and my badness gets out. They send me to the play place so I don't be bored. I ask Mr. Ted if he can tell my mum not to send me there. But she doesn't hear him. He is magic.

I wish I got to go back to my Nan's. My mum says I can't because my Nan is lazy and smells. She calls her bad words. I don't think she is lazy or smelly. But my mum gets mad when I tell her about it.

"That woman is not getting her hands on my children," she says. "She is poison."

I think my Nan is nice. But I am nearly nine years old. My mum says my Nan won't like me anymore because I am nearly all big. She only likes babies that she can manipulate, my mum says. So I have to go to the play place. I go on Thursday, Friday, Saturday and Sunday. Then I go back to my mum and dad's on Monday. I am not allowed to use the things in the house when I come home. She says I am not allowed to sit down. I have to get a bath. But I have to get the medicine first and make all the sick come out. Then I am not dirty on the inside or the outside.

I am allowed to go outside and play when I have had a bath. But I don't want to. Maybe I can lie down forever and go away. It feels all sad inside. Maybe my tummy wants to cry. I don't let the crying get out. I don't ever let my mum see it. Then she gets mad at me and tells me to stop being a baby about everything. I don't tell her about the play place. Then she will know I am bad.

I don't know why my mum sends me to the play place and not my brother. Maybe because he sleeps by the fire all day long. I wish my mum liked me and I could be good so she would keep me in the house. Lots of people come to the play place in the day time. Sometimes, they come at nighttime too and then, we have to get out of bed. But, mostly it is the day time. They hurt us all the time with the hurt thing.

We have to do the hurt thing to each other, sometimes. Then they take pictures about it. They make us smile. I don't like it. I don't like to do the hurt thing to other children. I don't like to make them cry. The people there say I have to. They smack me if I don't. They smack me if I take too long. I don't like when they smack me. They use a belt and then they do it millions of times until I fall over and nearly die.

I don't be able to stop the crying when I have to do the hurt thing. But I don't be able to stop. I am not allowed to. They tell me to stop the crying part or else. It makes my tummy want to be sick. I wish I got to go home. I try and wish my hardest but I don't ever go home. I wish I got to go away. I try to tell the people please in my head so they say it's okay. But they don't hear me. I tell the other children I am sorry.

I do the hurt part wrong, sometimes. I don't be very good at it. The people there tell me I am stupid. They are right. Stupid Boy. They get mad because I do it all wrong. I don't mean to. The man shows me how to do it properly. They do it very hard because it is my fault. I made them do it so they are going to make me remember. That is what the dark man said. He told me to do the hurt thing to a girl. But I didn't do it right. I didn't know what I was supposed to do. He called it words I didn't know.

The dark man smacked me because I didn't get it right. He told me not to dare cry about it. It was my fault he got to do the hurt thing to her. He told me I had to watch. He holded her hands down and did it. He did it very hard and she cried very bad. He got his hand on her neck I thought he was going to snap it away. But he didn't. It was all my fault. He told me to take her to the bathroom and get her cleaned up when he was finished. He told me to stop crying. They didn't want my stupid face all red. They took pictures in the bathroom. But I didn't be able to keep the crying away.

Then it was night time and they said I was bad. The dark man came in the room and he took me out. He put his thing in my mouth until it was all bad. I didn't let the sick out. But it wanted to come out. He asked me if I liked it. I said yes. But I didn't really. I didn't want him to get mad about it if I said no. But I didn't want the bad man to come because I told lies. I nodded my head and keeped the crying away.

The dark man taked me to another room after. He tied me on a chair. But, I falled to sleep. They did the hurt thing when I didn't know about it. He told me I better learn my lesson about doing the thing to other children. I told him I was sorry.

STUPID BOY

I don't ever tell anyone about the play place. Sometimes, I don't be able to stop the crying about it. I don't think about it. But then my eyes just cry on their own and I don't know how to stop them. I don't let anyone see. But sometimes people do. I tell them I don't feel very well. I don't want them to know that I am bad and I do bad things. I don't even tell Mr. Ted.

I wish in my tummy that I don't have to go back. Maybe God can take me away. I ask him about it too. But he doesn't ever. I ask him to make my brother better too. He has to go to the nice doctors. He sleeps lots of times. My mum says the doctor will make him better. It is because he is too scared to eat.

My mum asks me if she looks nice. I nod my head and tell her she is very pretty. I make a big smile and then she has a big smile too.

"Do you promise?" she asks me. I cross my heart and tell her I do.

My mum is excited about the doctor's. "He always keeps me in there," she says. "Then he can spend time with me." We wait for my dad. My mum always tells me about the nice doctor. My dad is going to the doctor's too. We get to the doctor's and I have to stay in the car.

I don't know what is happening. My dad comes out all fast. He is running. He doesn't say any words to me. He gets in the car and then we drive away. My brother isn't there. Maybe my mum went away with the doctor.

I ask my dad, but he doesn't say anything. I feel scared in my tummy about it. We drive to my Nan's house.

"Get out of the car," he says. I don't do it fast enough and he grabs my arm and pulls me out. I don't know what I did that was bad. I didn't let my badness out. My dad bangs on my Nan's door and then she answers it. They talk about my brother. I don't know what they say. He isn't very well.

"You can't go to the play place anymore," my dad shouts at me. "And I don't want to hear a thing about it."

My tummy does the turn over thing. I don't be able to stop my tummy from all shaking inside. I don't keep the crying away. My Nan hugs me all tight about it. The cries want to get out very bad and I don't be able to breathe. My dad runs back to the car and goes away.

"It'll be alright," my Nan says. "I'm sure he'll let you go back. He's just worried."

But I don't be sad about the play place.

STUPID BOY

Contact

dearmrted@gmail.com

http://jdstockholm.com/

http://www.facebook.com/dearmrted

These two sites have been invaluable to me throughout the last few years. I salute the many people on there, survivors, directors and above all, my friends. Thank you for the support at those times I needed it.

http://www.isurvive.org.uk

http://www.recoveryourlife.com/

Made in United States
North Haven, CT
14 July 2023